Linguistic Diversity and Teaching

REFLECTIVE TEACHING
AND THE SOCIAL CONDITIONS OF SCHOOLING

A Series for Prospective and Practicing Teachers
Daniel P. Liston and Kenneth M. Zeichner, Series Editors

Zeichner/Liston • Reflective Teaching: An Introduction

Liston/Zeichner • Culture and Teaching

Maher/Ward • Gender and Teaching

Commins/Miramontes • Linguistic Diversity and Teaching

Linguistic Diversity
and Teaching

Nancy L. Commins
University of Colorado at Denver

Ofelia B. Miramontes
University of Colorado

Routledge
Taylor & Francis Group
New York   London

First published by Lawrence Erlbaum Associates, Inc., Publishers
10 Industrial Avenue
Mahwah, New Jersey 07430

Reprinted 2009 by Routledge

Routledge

270 Madison Avenue
New York, NY 10016

2 Park Square, Milton Park
Abingdon, Oxon OX14 4RN, UK

Cover design by Kathryn Houghtaling Lacey

Library of Congress Cataloging-in-Publication Data

Commins, Nancy L.
  Linguistic diversity and teaching / Nancy L. Commins, Ofelia B. Miramontes.
    p.   cm. — (Reflective teaching and the social conditions of schooling)
  Includes bibliographical references and index.
  ISBN 0-8058-2736-6 (alk. paper)
    1. Native language and education—Case studies.   2. Education, Bilingual—Case studies.
I. Miramontes, Ofelia B.   II. Title.   III. Series.

LC201.5.C59   2005
370.117—dc22
                                                                2004062506
                                                                CIP

CONTENTS

II. PUBLIC ARGUMENTS   103

III. FINAL ARGUMENTS AND SOME SUGGESTIONS AND RESOURCES FOR FURTHER REFLECTION   137

SERIES PREFACE

AN ESSENTIAL SERIES INTRODUCTION

Whereas many readers rarely read introductory material, we hope you will continue. The success of this book depends, in large part, on how you use it. In what follows we outline some of our key assumptions and we suggest ways for approaching the material in each book of this series entitled, "Reflective Teaching and the Social Conditions of Schooling." First we identify some of our reasons for creating this series. We then relate a bit about our dissatisfaction with how teacher education is usually conducted and how it can be changed. Finally we outline suggestions for ways to best utilize the material in this and subsequent texts.

Some years ago we were asked to develop further the ideas outlined in our book *Teacher Education and the Social Conditions of Schooling* (Liston & Zeichner, 1991). It was suggested that we take our basic approach to teacher reflection and our ideas about teacher education curricula and put them into practice. The proposal was attractive and the subsequent endeavor proved to be very challenging. It never seems easy to translate educational "shoulds" and possibilities into schooling "cans" and realities. But we think (and we hope) we have made progress in that effort by designing a series of books intended to help prospective, beginning, and experienced teachers to reflect on their profession, their teaching, and their experiences. We are pleased and delighted to have the opportunity to share this work with you. We hope you will find these texts to be engaging and useful.

We are two university teacher educators, both former elementary teachers, who have worked in inner-city, small town, and suburban elementary and middle schools. We are committed to public schools as democratic institutions, as places of learning in which people of all walks of life come to learn how to live together in a democratic society. Although we are personally committed to ways of working and living together that are much more collaborative than exist today—we are educators first, realists second, and dreamers third. It is our firm belief that an education that engages prospective and practicing teachers' heads and hearts, their beliefs and passions, needs to be fair and honest. We have neither written nor encouraged others to write these texts to convince you to see schools and society in a particular light, but rather to engage you in a consideration of crucial issues that all teachers need to address. Once engaged we hope that you will be better able to articulate your views, responses, and responsibilities to students and parents, and come to better understand aspects of your role as a teacher in a democratic society.

IMPACTS OF THE SOCIAL CONDITIONS OF SCHOOLING

Prospective teachers need to be prepared for the problems and challenges of public schooling. Sometimes the focus in schools (departments and colleges) of education remains strictly on the processes that occur within the classroom and inside the school walls. At times, teacher education programs emphasize instructional methodology and the psychology of the learner in university course work and underscore survival strategies for student teaching. These are certainly important elements in any teacher's preparation and ones that cannot be ignored. But classrooms and schools are not insulated environments. What goes on inside schools is greatly influenced by what occurs outside of schools. The students who attend and the teachers and administrators who work within those walls bring into the school building all sorts of cultural assumptions, social influences, and contextual dynamics. Unless some concerted attention is given to those assumptions, influences, and dynamics, to the reality of school life and to the social conditions of schooling, our future teachers will be ill prepared.

Over the last 10 years, teacher educators have paid greater attention to the social conditions of schooling. But a consensus of opinion on this issue does not exist. The professional aspects of teacher education, including attention to the social conditions of schooling, have been criticized by scholars and politicians such as those associated with the Fordham Foundation who believe that content knowledge alone is sufficient to teach. While we recognize the importance of teachers' content knowledge, this view is, we believe, a gross and politically motivated mistake that will do harm to the students in our public schools and their teachers. Students need teachers who have the professional preparation necessary to teach a greatly diverse student population to achieve high academic standards. We hope that the books in this series will contribute to this end.

We are living in a time of remarkable change, a time of social and political transformation. In an era that is rife with social controversies and political difficulties, in which public schooling has increasingly come under attack, during which we are seeing marked changes in this country's cultural demographic make-up, in which there are great pressures to transform public schools into private, for-profit enterprises, we must educate well our teaching workforce. Future teachers cannot, on their own, solve the many societal issues confronting the schools, but they should certainly know what those issues are, have a sense of their own beliefs about those issues, and understand the many ways in which those issues will come alive within their school's walls. Poverty and wealth, our culture of consumerism, what seems to be an increasing amount of violent behavior, and the work pressures of modern life affect the children who attend our public schools. Public attitudes about competition and excellence, race and ethnicity, gender roles and homosexuality, and the environment affect students inside and outside of schools. One can be certain that the issues that affect all of our lives outside of schools will certainly influence students inside their schools.

EXAMINING THE SOCIAL CONDITIONS OF SCHOOLING

Probably the best way to begin to examine contextual issues such as these is to be "attentive" early on in one's professional preparation, to experience features of the social conditions of schooling, and then to examine the experience and what we know about the social and cultural context of schooling. We encourage prospective and practicing teachers to do this. But teacher preparation programs often are not organized in a fashion that would encourage the discussion and examination of these sorts of shared experiences. What traditionally are called *social foundations* courses are typically not school-based, but set apart from some of the more realistic, practical, and engaged dilemmas of schooling. In schools of education we frequently teach what the sociology or philosophy of education has to say about schools but we tend to teach it as sociologists or philosophers, not as teachers struggling with crucial and highly controversial issues. Thus, in our own work with prospective and practicing teachers we have developed ways to examine contextual issues of schooling and to enable ourselves and students to articulate our ideas, beliefs, theories, and feelings about those issues. The books in this series attempt to utilize some of these insights and to pass along to others the content and the processes we have found useful.

When students and faculty engage in discussions of the social and political conditions of schooling and the effects of these conditions on students and schools, it is likely that the talk will be lively and controversies will emerge. In this arena there are no absolutely "right" or "wrong" answers. There are choices, frequently difficult ones, choices that require considerable discussion, deliberation, and justification. In order for these discussions to occur we need to create classroom settings that are conducive to conversations about difficult and controversial issues. The best format for such discussion is not the debate, the (in)formal argument, or dispassionate and aloof analysis. Instead the most conducive environment is a classroom designed to create dialogue and conversation among participants with differing points of view. There isn't a recipe or formula that will ensure this type of environment but we think the following suggestions are worth considering.

It is important for individuals using these texts to engage in discussions that are sensitive and respectful toward others, and at the same time challenge each other's views. This is not an easy task. It requires each participant to come to the class sessions prepared, to listen attentively to other people's views, and to address one another with a tone and attitude of respect. This means that when disagreements between individuals occur, and they inevitably will occur, each participant should find a way to express that disagreement without diminishing or attacking the other individual. Participants in these professional discussions need to be able to voice their views freely and to be sensitive toward others. Frequently, this is difficult to do. In discussions of controversial issues, ones that strike emotional chords, we are prone to argue in a way that belittles or disregards another person and their point of view. At times, we try to dismiss both the claim and the person. But if the discussions that these books help to initiate are carried on in that demeaning fashion, the potential power of these works will not be realized. A discussion of this paragraph should occur before discussing the substance raised by this particular text. It is our conviction that when a class keeps both substance and pedagogy in the forefront it has a way of engaging individuals in a much more positive manner. From our own past experiences, we have found that during the course of a class's use of this material it may be quite helpful to pause and focus on substantive and pedagogical issues in a conscious and forthright manner. Such time is generally well spent.

UNDERSTANDING AND EXAMINING PERSONAL BELIEFS ABOUT TEACHING AND SCHOOLING

It is also our belief that many educational issues engage and affect our heads and our hearts. Teaching is work that entails both thinking and feeling; those who can reflectively think and feel will find their work more rewarding and their efforts more successful. Good teachers find ways to listen to and integrate their passions, beliefs, and judgments. And so we encourage not only the type of group deliberation just outlined but also an approach to reading that is attentive to an individual's felt sense or what some might call "gut" level reactions. In the books in this series that contain case material and written reactions to that material, along with the public arguments that pertain to the issues raised, we believe it is essential that you, the reader, attend to your felt reactions, and attempt to sort out what those reactions tell you. At times it seems we can predict our reactions to the readings and discussions of this material while at other times it can invoke reactions and feelings that surprise us. Attending to those issues in a heartfelt manner, one that is honest and forthright, gives us a better sense of ourselves as teachers and our understandings of the world. Not only do students walk into schools with expectations and assumptions formed as a result of life experiences but so do their teachers. Practicing and prospective teachers can benefit from thinking about their expectations and assumptions. Hopefully, our work will facilitate this sort of reflection.

ABOUT THE BOOKS IN THIS SERIES

The first work in this series, *Reflective Teaching*, introduces the notion of teacher reflection and develops it in relation to the social conditions of schooling. Building on this concept, the second work in the series, *Culture and Teaching*, encourages a reflection on and examination of diverse cultures and schooling. In *Gender and Teaching*, the third work in the series, Frinde Maher and Janie Ward examine the central role of gender in both teaching and schooling. And in this volume Nancy Commins and Ofelia Miramontes offer both an in-depth and a bird's eye view of linguistic diversity in today's schools. These two experts, known nationally for their scholarly and practical contributions to the education of English language learners, enable us to see this complex arena more clearly. Commins and Miramontes convey many of the central issues that attend learning and linguistic diversity in our schools. We are lucky to have these two individuals as our guides.

SERIES ACKNOWLEDGMENTS

Two individuals have been essential to the conception and execution of this series. Kathleen Keller, our first editor at St. Martin's Press (where the series originated), initially suggested that we further develop the ideas outlined in *Teacher Education and the Social Conditions of Schooling* (Liston & Zeichner, 1991). Kathleen was very helpful in the initial stages of this effort and we wish to thank her for that. Naomi Silverman, our current and beloved editor at Lawrence Erlbaum Associates, has patiently and skillfully prodded us along attending to both the "big picture" and the small details. She has been remarkably supportive and capably informative. We are very thankful and indebted to Naomi.

—*Daniel P. Liston*
—*Kenneth M. Zeichner*

PREFACE

A work focused on linguistic diversity and teaching can evoke strong reactions. Demographics indicate that there has been, and will continue to be, a significant increase in the number of students who come from linguistic backgrounds other than English in our public schools. The increase in linguistic diversity has occurred without a commensurate rise in the number of ethnic minority and bilingual teachers. Monolingual English speaking teachers often find themselves doubtful, apprehensive, and uncertain about their roles and responsibilities with regard to such learners.

Issues surrounding new English learners exist within a highly charged political and social climate. They involve not only language, but also culture, class, ethnicity, and the persistent inequities that characterize our educational system. It is easy to see how the presence of English language learners can make teachers feel inadequate or uncomfortable since most teachers in the United States are native English speakers, who have been prepared to teach native English speakers in English. Because linguistic diversity is also so closely linked with issues of culture, class, race, and even gender there are no simple or easy answers to the questions that arise. The central theme of this text is to raise the questions, and provide a context for reflection regarding these issues. Because there is a tremendous variety in the circumstances of new English learners and of how their presence interfaces with the communities to which they arrive, there are many questions that arise and the answers are far from simple. It is our intention to provide various perspectives on how to address these challenges. We include our own views, but they are just our version of truth and we invite further reaction and interpretation.

Linguistic diversity receives little, if any, attention in the majority of teacher education programs. To address linguistic diversity is more than just how to teach second language learners. Linguistic diversity includes a full spectrum of language proficiencies including monolingual English speakers, students who are just beginning to learn in two languages, as well as those students who have already made significant progress towards academic proficiency in both. To become prepared to address linguistic diversity is to learn about how to create schools that address the full spectrum of language proficiency and that provide an equitable education to all.

No matter what your beliefs are, it is essential that you enter the teaching profession not only with a set of techniques and strategies, but also with an awareness of the external social conditions of your students and how you are responding to them. Any technique or strategy can only be successful to the extent that it is appropriately situated in the cultural, linguistic, and class reality of the students you are teaching. We believe that teachers can play a significant role in addressing the inequities in the educational system that often characterize the schooling of language minority students.

We hope that the combination of the cases in the book and the discussions that follow will help you to begin to evolve your own practical theories, explore and perhaps modify some of your basic beliefs and assumptions and become acquainted with other points of view. This is not an easy or trivial process. This book is not about the right way to think, but rather about examining how the way we think influences our actions in the classroom and beyond. As the other authors in this series argue, theories and beliefs are grounded in our past experiences, our received knowledge, and our basic values. As we reflect, we can discover things that may confirm our view of the world, others that surprise us, and still others that challenge our assumptions about ourselves. These reflections hopefully will enable you, as an educator, to act with greater clarity.

CONTENT AND STRUCTURE

Like the other books in this series *Culture and Teaching* (Liston & Zeichner, 1996) and *Gender and Teaching* (Maher & Ward, 2002) this book is organized into three basic parts. Part I consists of four cases dealing with aspects of linguistic diversity and teaching, along with a range of preservice and practicing teachers' and administrators' reactions to each case. Part II is an elaboration of three public arguments pertaining to the issues raised in the cases in Part I. Part III presents our own concluding statement about some of the issues raised throughout the volume, additional exercises for reflection, and a bibliography of resources.

The Case Studies

The cases in Part I explore different aspects of the impacts of the changing demographics of public schools. Four case studies are presented. All of them highlight situations monolingual English speaking, Euro American teachers might face within the context of schools that serve a linguistically diverse student body. One of them also delves a little deeper into a student's reality outside the school setting. The cases are composites of our own personal experiences in observing students and staff in our roles as teachers, teachers on special assignments, district level administrators and university professors in teacher preparation programs. They also include the experiences shared by practicing teachers, district personnel, as well as pre-service and practicing teachers in districts across the country.

In Case 1 "The Cycle: Frank and Vu" we examine one teacher's experience in trying to respond to the needs of a second language learner without adequate information or background knowledge about what to do. In Case 2 "Marisa's Prospects" we focus on a junior high learner and her teacher who makes an extra effort to reach out to the student and her family. In doing so, this teacher revises many of her prior assumptions. In Case 3 "Friendship, Professionalism and Programs" we highlight one teacher's attempt to make changes to the structure of her school whose student population has changed dramatically over several years. Her struggle over what to do calls into question some of her prior experiences, and also puts her in potential conflict with many of her colleagues. In Case 4 "What is Equal Treatment?" we explore the issue of assessment and how increasing linguistic diversity challenges teachers to find appropriate assessments that meet the needs of students and still fit into the accountability systems districts currently have in place.

Each case study is followed by a set of reactions written by prospective and practicing teachers and administrators whom we asked to read and respond to these stories. They represent only some of the many and diverse ways in which people both inside and outside of school systems react to and deal with these issues. Reading their reactions, we can see not only the complexities of these problems and of other people's responses, but we can also perhaps further understand and refine our own positions.

Between each case study and the reactions, and after the set of reactions for each case study, we have left space in the text for you to write your own reactions and reflections. People approach this task differently. Some find it easier to write their reactions after reading the case study; others find it helpful to wait until they have read others' reactions. We suggest jotting down your reactions in both places. Because the process of learning and reflection is unpredictable and changing, we want to encourage you to make a record of your development over time, as you change your mind, see new perspectives, perhaps change your mind back again, perhaps move in a different direction. We want to encourage you to explore as many different approaches as possible, in response to the case studies, the readers' responses, and your own initial reactions.

The Public Arguments

In Part II we move from the particular realm of the case studies to the more general arena of public arguments and present three very different views about linguistic diversity, teaching, and education. What we call "public arguments" or "public voices" represent clusters of orientations organized around general values rather than sets of hard and fast principles to which all who speak in that "voice" must adhere. These summaries represent some basic assumptions that guide their proponents' perspectives on educational polices related to issues of linguistic diversity. We present three views that diverge greatly in how best to teach second language learners of English. They include those who feel English should be the only language of instruction, those who feel all children should receive instruction in both their first language and English, and those who reject some, and accept other, aspects of the each of the two other arguments. We hope that our combination of case studies and public arguments will help our readers explore these ramifications on many different levels as they come to locate themselves and others within these debates.

Our Own Views

Finally, in Part III we offer our own readings of the issues associated with linguistic diversity and teaching and outline a number of ways in which practicing and prospective teachers can continue to explore these topics. We offer an introduction to our own perspective, one that embraces linguistic diversity as a positive contribution to the nation's schools. Ultimately we take the position that our schools are places where various forms of inequality flourish. By challenging these inequalities a teacher can build an empowering education for all children. But, again, ours are only two views, and we encourage you to develop your own. At the end of this section we outline some suggestions for further explorations and provide a bibliography of both the sources cited in this book and additional readings that we consider essential for any teacher's professional library.

ACKNOWLEDGMENTS

We are deeply indebted to the teachers, administrators, and students who contributed directly to this book. By sharing their challenges and rewards, their thoughts, analyses, deliberations, experiences and wisdom on a variety of issues relating to linguistic diversity, they have allowed us to broaden our thinking and understanding of these issues.

We have not acknowledged each of them by name for fear of leaving someone out, but have been faithful in presenting their individual voices. We are indebted to them not only for their responses to the cases but also for their encouragement throughout our writing process. We are continually inspired by their excellent work with linguistically diverse students.

We especially want to thank Dan Liston for his unfailing support, gentle reminders, and incisive comments on the cases and the manuscript. Our series editors Dan Liston and Ken Zeichner have a long-standing commitment and understanding of linguistic diversity as a vital issue in teacher education. We very much appreciate their encouragement, support, and inclusion of this book in their series. Our special thanks to Naomi Silverman our editor at LEA, for her constant optimism and her advocacy for this important issue and for our project in particular. We also thank Sue Hopewell and Suzanne Sawyer-Ratliff for their reading and comments on the final draft.

From Nancy: I want to dedicate my work to Ofelia who has profoundly influenced who I am both professionally and personally. I especially thank her for having the confidence in me to see this project through. I would not be who I am today without Ofelia's friendship and guidance. My gratitude to Ken and Alex Saul who make everything I do possible by their unconditional love and support.

From Ofelia: I want to dedicate my work to the linguistically diverse students and the teachers, administrators and teacher education students who have committed their energies, intelligence, and care to this vital area of education. And, to my friend Nancy with whom I have the wonderful good fortune to work with over the past 20 years. This project would not have been possible without Nancy's knowledge, commitment, love, and caring. My husband Bill's constancy and support have provided the foundation for tackling important and challenging projects. My love always.

I

CASE STUDIES
AND REACTIONS

INTRODUCTION TO CASE 1

This case focuses on the difficulties that arise when teachers are unaware that the needs of linguistically diverse students may differ from those of native speakers of English. When they lack information about what types of instruction students are actually receiving in different settings, teachers can seriously misjudge the academic progress being made by students. Even when teachers are supportive and well intentioned, a lack of knowledge about second language development and appropriate strategies that help second language learners succeed can lead to disappointment, frustration, and anger. You will see the consequences of founding hopes and expectations for student performance on faulty assumptions. Specifically, the case describes what happens when a fourth grade teacher with limited experiences with second language learners acts in ways that to him seem logical when making decisions about what is best for one of his students.

Questions that are raised in this case include: What is the relationship between expectations and appropriate instruction? What understandings do teachers need in order to teach students learning English as a second language effectively? What are the consequences of fragmented instructional programs? What kind of instruction leads to competence over time? How can communication be fostered in a school?

1

CASE 1: "THE CYCLE: FRANK AND VU"

Frank is a hard working and conscientious fourth grade teacher at Walnut Elementary. He prepares carefully for his students and always tries to take into account students' individual needs. He feels he gives students choices, supports them in their learning, and provides a caring environment in his classroom. This year for the first time Frank has a student in his class who is an English second language learner, Vu. Vu has been in the United States for a year and a half.

Frank has thought a lot about Vu's educational needs. What has concerned him lately, however, is why Vu doesn't always take advantage of the range of activities Frank provides in the classroom. He has noticed that Vu is often alone and doesn't always seem to know what's going on. Frank remembers talking to Roger the special education teacher who had told him that given the short time Vu has been in the country he was fairly sure it was an issue of English second language development. He told Frank that the best first step was to talk with Betsy, the English as a Second Language (ESL) teacher.

Betsy is very helpful. She talks to Frank about the fact that Vu is probably having difficulty understanding all that was being said to him. She gives Frank an example by taking a simple picture book and describing and discussing the contents with him in Spanish. Although Frank had taken 2 years of Spanish in high school, and certainly understands what is going on in the pictures, he eventually tunes out Betsy's description because he is only picking up a word here and there. When she asks him a question about something on one of the pages he is caught off guard, embarrassed, and frustrated. At that moment he realizes some of what Vu must be experiencing.

Betsy suggests that Frank send Vu to her ESL classes where, she tells him, she uses particular techniques to help second language learners develop proficiency in English. These she says include using lots of pictures and actual objects to make vocabulary explicit, presenting lessons with many visuals and clear language, and giving her students an opportunity to practice their English skills in a safe environment. She offers to work with Frank to help him develop some of these techniques himself so that he can support Vu and other second language learners he might have in the future directly in their classroom activities. She also tells him that because she sees students for only an hour or so per day, these students also need consistent support from their classroom teachers in order to succeed in the other 4 to 5 hours they spend there. That makes sense to Frank.

Frank and Betsy also talk briefly about how the community around the school is changing and how all of the teachers will need some ESL training for the growing number of second language students in the school. Betsy is skeptical that this will happen. Frank fears that if no training is made available to the teachers, it will really limit student learning. But he knows Betsy is right about the lack of attention to this issue and about the resistance within the staff to making changes. Several teachers on the staff don't feel it's their job to know about English language development for second language learners. Some of Frank's colleagues think that going to ESL classes is a waste of time. They believe that if students are simply in an all English environment all day they will learn English. Others feel that it is more important for students to stay in their own classroom rather than being pulled-out for instruction. Still others send students to ESL begrudgingly or leave the choice up to the students. After talking to Betsy and experiencing his own discomfort in another language, he is convinced Vu needs a different approach to learning in English and special attention to English language development. Although his conversation with Betsy did not give him a full picture of what is taught in the ESL curriculum, he has confidence in Betsy and trusts her judgment about its value. He is convinced it is a very important and basic part of Vu's instruction and makes sure Vu goes regularly.

The ESL program at Walnut Elementary is run on a pullout basis. Students across the school are scheduled into Betsy's classroom by levels of English proficiency. For example, she has an hour period in which she works with beginning level students across the grades. At a different time of the day she works with more advanced students. Although Betsy knows it is important to coordinate her instruction with the classroom teachers, the number of student she needs to serve has grown yearly and she now finds little time to coordinate services. She has also heard the same comments about ESL that Frank has. She has found that most teachers in the building consider her program an intrusion into their day, and they are not particularly open to meeting with her. She worries that as the second language learner population grows, the necessary teacher training will not be provided and more and more students will begin to have trouble in their classes.

Vu goes to ESL during Frank's reading and language arts period. This seems reasonable because Vu's limited English made it difficult for him to understand many of the words he tried to read. But, because Vu is not part of Frank's reading and language arts instruction, Frank does not know how Vu's literacy and language skills are developing. Although he has meant to talk to Betsy and to learn more about second language instruction, in reality he never seems to be able to find the time.

Betsy's program focuses on oral language development. She feels that it is critical for students to be comfortable and competent in using English orally. She knows that building a strong background in the sounds, syntax, and semantics of English allows students to move into reading with greater ease and real understanding. Her hard work with Vu is paying off. He learns new English vocabulary quickly, is understanding more and more ideas, and because he is a bright, friendly, and outgoing youngster, his oral English has developed quickly. He is now also very interested in looking through English books and figuring out words in the text.

Frank's communication with Betsy indicates that Vu is making excellent progress. He is now able to understand simple lessons. He can tell because Vu is gaining a great deal of confidence. He can answer basic questions and will even ask for clarification of information that he doesn't understand. Vu's vocabulary is increasing steadily and he can now tell a story about something that happened at home or in the community with little hesitation. By the middle of the year Vu is interacting comfortably with other students in his classes and has really opened up. Frank sees how well Vu is able to communicate with his classmates and how they have come to like and accept him. He thinks its time for Vu to spend more time with his class and approaches Betsy about having Vu stay in the classroom rather than going to ESL.

Betsy does not believe Vu is ready. She knows he is only just beginning to read in English with a second language approach that allows her to closely monitor his comprehension There are still many ideas which are difficult for him to understand because he is unfamiliar with the language. For example, she has organized her curriculum around science units. Recently they had discussed the idea of transformation of matter. Using a very hands-on approach she had demonstrated the transformation of water from solid to liquid to gas. The students enjoyed the activity but when she asked them to describe what had happened and why they thought it had happened, she realized that they were not able to articulate what they had done and seen. She decided then to focus her next few lessons on teaching her students how to express these ideas—that is, how to talk about the ideas and processes themselves rather than simply just listening and nodding their heads. By the end of the next week, her group was able to have a clear and lively discussion about the experiment using words like transformation, solids, liquids, and so on, which had been new to them. They could also ask each other questions about the topic, answer them with confidence, and write about their experience and observations with her help. She feels Vu still needs more of these focused experiences on a regular basis.

Betsy tries to explain this to Frank and adds that although she feels Vu has made good progress she knows there are several major areas in which Vu needs instructional support. She places a big emphasis on oral language because it is important that English language learners have a strong listening and speaking background in their second language. They need to become comfortable with English sounds, vocabulary, and oral expression as they work to make meaning from the material they read. For this reason he has not yet received much direct reading instruction. Although he has made great strides, his limited vocabulary and his lack of familiarity with topics in English cause him difficulty in understanding content area material. Literacy skills are critical in fourth grade and Vu will need help in developing those reading skills. In addition, his vocabulary is still pretty basic and he will need help in developing comprehension to a fourth grade level in English reading.

Betsy points out once again that using English as a second language methods to help Vu continue his strong development is very important. She explains that research demonstrates that although English language learners can pick up face-to-face interpersonal communication skills quickly, these skills represent only a surface knowledge of the language and that for Vu to be able to do all his class work without ESL support will be very difficult for him. Frank admits he doesn't have any experience with ESL methods. He has also never been involved in initial reading instruction and is not sure how to approach a beginning reader, but he has created an inviting classroom environment and he thinks Vu's enthusiasm for English books will carry them through.

Betsy remains ambivalent. It is true that she has had a couple of students who have made great progress when they returned to their classroom full time, although this is rare. Because Frank is offering to provide Vu some direct one-on-one support, and given how well Vu is fitting in with the other students in his class perhaps it could work. She has an overload of students and perhaps the one-on-one help Frank has promised could benefit Vu. Betsy knows that Frank is a good teacher and that Vu is anxious to be with his class. Frank's enthusiasm for working with Vu is hard for Betsy to resist. She recognizes that Vu is a very bright and motivated student. Could she be limiting his opportunities as Frank insists? In the end she agrees to have Vu leave ESL classes and sets aside her uneasiness about the difficulties she knows Vu will encounter trying to deal with fourth grade content, ideas, and reading without support focused directly on his needs as a second language learner.

Frank is excited and looking forward to having Vu back in class. Because he knows Vu has not had extensive English reading instruction, he puts him in one of his lower reading groups. He feels that this way Vu will not have to compete at too high a level at the beginning. His hopes are high. Vu seems happy to be back in the classroom full time. For the first several weeks things go well. The other children in the class are ready to help Vu when he needs it and things seem to be working. Over the next month, however, Vu seems to be more and more frustrated when others try to help him. He is no longer eager for others to help him and seems more and more withdrawn.

Frank also notices that Vu is really struggling with the work in reading. During the reading period he spends a great deal of time getting up, talking to other students, or wandering around the classroom. In the reading group he fidgets, never seems to be in the right place on the page, and has difficulty answering questions put to him about the story. Although Frank tries to explain the ideas reflected in the text to him, Vu doesn't seem to understand and often answers questions with irrelevant information. He works with Vu individually as often as possible, but it is often only one or two days per week for brief periods of time. At the last parent conference, Vu's parents expressed some concern that their son was not as enthusiastic about school as he had been, and on some days did not even want to come to school. They were very worried about this change in attitude and wondered if anything had happened at school to cause it. Frank explained the change in Vu's schedule and how he believed this would benefit Vu in the long run. Vu's parents had said they trusted Frank's decision and they would help Vu as much as possible.

As time goes on Vu does not seem to be making any better progress. In fact, he often does not pay attention to what the group is engaged in, and when called on he gets very frustrated. He has begun to distract other students, will sit at his desk just looking at his work, and gets very little accomplished. Frank feels that he has bent over backwards to try to help Vu get ahead. He is particularly disappointed to see Vu's lack of motivation, and the constant disruptions he initiates in class. Frank knows Vu's parents are not literate in English and can't help him with his English homework. Frank knows, however, that they are encouraging him to do his best in school and he is grateful for that. Frank feels guilty that although he has tried to work with Vu individually, he has only been able to do so a couple of times per week. Even in these sessions, Vu does not seem engaged. Maybe he was totally wrong about Vu's potential. Although he hates to admit it, Vu's behavior makes him angry. The students in Frank's class also seem to have turned against Vu. In picking teams for games, he is almost always the last one chosen. Frank has also heard a couple of students tease Vu about his reading ability.

Now he is trying to decide what he should do next. He had been so confident that the good feelings and the strong classroom environment he had established for students would be enough for Vu to succeed. He wonders if he has ignored some of the basic principles that Betsy had insisted were known to be necessary for second language English learners to succeed? Were methods of presentation really so important? He knows it was unfair to blame to Vu and to question his potential but he can't help it. He also knows that it is very difficult for him to determine whether Vu's problems in the classroom come from his frequent academic failures, his treatment by his classmates, or Frank's own feelings of disappointment that he is sure are probably being communicated to Vu. Could this all be part of the isolation Vu is feeling because of a lack of proficiency in English—not understanding all of the content being read or explained in class or difficulty in expressing ideas? He recalls the frustration and anger on Vu's face when, in trying to participate with the class, he had launched into an explanation and then got stuck in the middle. That makes Frank remember his own experience with Betsy.

Frank decides he needs to rethink his decision. If he goes to talk with Betsy would she say, "I told you so"? It is hard for him to believe that her classes could really make such a difference. And, given the number of students she is now serving what if she isn't able to take Vu back into her class? Even if Vu could get back into ESL that would only be for an hour a day. What is he going to do to help Vu for all of the time Vu is in his class? Is he blaming Vu for his own inability to find the time to teach him appropriately? Even with ESL classes, it is *his* classroom where much of the negativity toward Vu has been created. Can he reestablish his relationship with Vu? Can he regain his trust, undo the negativity that has been created in Vu's school life? Frank very much wants to be part of Vu's learning. He is looking for guidance about what to do next.

How would you advise him to proceed with Betsy? How about with Vu?

READER REACTIONS TO FRANK'S SITUATION

REACTIONS TO "THE CYCLE: FRANK AND VU"

The differing perspectives of the respondents to this case reflect the complexity of the issues surrounding linguistic diversity. Some readers focused on Frank's actions; others commented on what was happening (or wasn't) in the school as a whole. They touched on the apparent lack of communication among staff members and time for collaboration. There were many opinions about role definitions and the need for formalized structures for collaboration among teachers if students like Vu are to be better served. Some pointed to the absence of the principal and questioned the lack of leadership regarding these issues. In addition, questions were raised about the lack of delineated policies for identification, placement, and criteria for ending second language support (exit criteria).

Another major theme among the responses to the case was how important it is for classroom teachers to understand the nature of second language development. Without these understandings, teachers are likely to overlook students' need for particular kinds of instruction. Nearly all the respondents felt it was the classroom teachers' responsibility to acquire the strategies necessary to ensure academic success.

Finally, respondents focused on the relationship between Frank and Vu and how important it would be for Vu's voice to be heard in the conversation regarding what was best for him. Several suggestions were offered in terms of how to build stronger and safer classroom communities.

Focus on Frank

Responses to Frank's actions varied. Many applauded him for at least trying to do something. They saw Vu as fortunate that Frank was willing to work with the ESL teacher and use this collaboration as a learning experience for other teachers. Others saw him as a victim of his ego and thought that he should put aside his pride and admit that he made a mistake. This would allow him to continue to collaborate with the ESL teacher to provide for Vu's individual needs.

> I admire his skills for reflection and self-evaluation. Frank is able to see what works in his teaching, and what needs to change. He is willing to change and learn according to the needs of his students, and this is what matters most. It seems that Frank is constantly asking himself what he could

do better and what instruction is in the best interest of his students. Frank is very present with his students and has good intentions.

—Second Year Elementary Bilingual Teacher

Frank did feel like Vu had certain academic shortcomings, but instead of immediately jumping to that conclusion, Frank actually took the time to consult his colleagues, which I found to be refreshing. Many teachers wouldn't have even taken the time to go through these steps to find out why a child is struggling.

—Prospective Teacher

Vu's educational opportunities take precedence over any feelings of guilt or awkwardness that Frank may experience. Further, Frank must come to see these events as a valuable learning experience and readily seek ways of improving Vu's daily schooling experience as soon as possible. The focus at this point should not be on determining fault, but rather on how everyone involved can help Vu to recover his initial feelings of being successful in his English language, social, and academic development.

—Elementary Teacher

I do think that Frank made a bad judgment call by pulling Vu so quickly out of the ESL program. But with the child's future at stake it is not too late to admit an error and send him back. Frank really needs to figure out what is best for Vu and shouldn't spend time dreading an "I told you so" from Betsy. Everyone makes mistakes and as professionals they should be able to deal with this issue in an adult manner. Betsy is really as much to blame for she approved the transition in the first place.

—Elementary Teacher

I think that Frank has just suffered from a case of super-teacher syndrome. We have all done it. This is when a teacher feels that he or she can take on a problem student and make huge strides and accomplishments that no one else could in a short period of time. This, of course, rarely happens in the real world.

—Elementary Teacher

I think that Frank's answer is obvious, and I think Frank already knows what that answer is: He must put his own pride on the shelf and ask Betsy for her help again. For a conscientious, reflective teacher like Frank, the students' needs must always come first. Frank realizes that he is not able to give Vu the type of support that he needs, and I commend him for being reflective enough of his own teaching to make that realization. Now he just has to act on his observations and do what is best for Vu, which is to get him back into his ESL class as soon as possible.

Although I disagree with Frank's initial decision to pull Vu out of his ESL classes, I can understand his feelings. Many teachers are uncomfortable about pullout classes, because they aren't sure about what goes on in these classes. Frank's decision to pull Vu out of his ESL class was made out of his desire to become more involved in Vu's education and I cannot fault him for his enthusiasm. However, I do feel that Frank has let the situation go on too long. He began realizing that he was not meeting Vu's needs and that Vu was acting poorly because of it fairly soon after he pulled Vu from his ESL class. I know that Frank was hopeful that the situation would improve in time, but I think that he has let his own pride confuse his judgment. As teachers we are often looked to as experts and it can be difficult to admit when we are wrong. But, it is time for Frank to admit his mistake and ask Betsy for her help with Vu.

—Elementary Teacher

Widening the Lens: Focus on the School

It is very difficult for a staff to achieve academic success for all its students without shared beliefs, a common philosophy, and a set of procedures based on them. Many saw Frank's actions as situated in a larger context where such agreements were lacking. They did not see him as the source of the problem, but rather the problem was caused by the lack of communication and collaboration in the school as a whole.

Faculty members with different backgrounds and training often disagree about what each teacher's role should be, as well as about what students should be taught in different settings. With the ever-increasing responsibilities being placed on teachers, it can be overwhelming to meet every student's needs within the time constraints of the school day. Power struggles are often reduced to "Which teacher is best?" rather than "What does the student need?" This conflict is exacerbated by the difficulties inherent in a pullout program, especially one that is not well coordinated with grade level instruction.

Teachers, regardless of background, need to be encouraged to share in the partnership of providing our children with the best educational practice. Consequently, there needs to be open communication and an informed, respectful understanding of the instructional methodologies that occur in each learning environment. To provide the students with learning experiences that are of the utmost in value, as teachers we need to communicate with one another and share our goals and focuses for our children.

—Student in Master's Program

Vu needs the assistance of a professional trained in English language acquisition, AS WELL AS, his classroom. Education is the most effective when it is a team effort, and everyone involved has an opinion of what a particular child needs. Frank tried to do it all on his own, and in the end, this "overachiever-super-teacher" attitude backfired on him.

—Second Year Elementary Bilingual Teacher

ESL teachers have so many children to service per day, limited hours to accomplish it all, and only so many battles that they can wage against skeptics on the merit and importance of ESL. Consequently, Betsy's superhero façade gives way to the realistic image of ONE soldier waging a DAILY battle against opposition.

—Graduate Student

Herein resides the resistance displayed by teachers with regards to truly addressing the needs of linguistically diverse students. We find that our ability to change is essential to being effective for our ever-changing student population. We question whether or not we are responsible for educating most of our students or all of our students. We find that we are actually quite parallel to the role of being a "learner" and rarely can rely upon being an expert in our profession. We find that asking for help and collaborating with knowledgeable and experienced colleagues is both humbling and transformative for us and for our students.

—Teacher

I find this case to be a bit disturbing. One thing which I have trouble understanding is the animosity that develops between the ESL specialist and classroom teachers. I've witnessed this in my practicum placements. I sincerely believe that all teachers should work together to benefit the students. The most important aspect of being a teacher is to educate students. I find it offensive that teachers would refuse to further educate themselves in order to benefit the students. . . . But one thing that I've come to recognize is that different students often succeed with different teaching techniques. . . . When some teachers send students to ESL begrudgingly or leave the choice up to the students, this indirectly belittles the importance of learning English and undermines the work of their teammates.

—Prospective Teacher

Leadership

Several respondents questioned the absence of the principal's voice in these conversations. They wondered why it was left up to Betsy and Frank to solve the problem. Leadership problems at the building level can result from a lack of guidance from the district about policies and procedures, as well as instructional approaches. In a well-run system, individual teachers shouldn't have been making these kinds of decisions on their own. On the other hand, they also felt that in the absence of such guidance, teachers still must act.

> Where is the building leader here? I see a lack of leadership, [a leader who] does not know about the changes that are occurring in school demographics, student needs and staff needs. The case spells out the need to come together as a staff and to create a vision to promote and support students. The need to restructure the school to become an ESL school instead of a small program within a school. This means involving everyone! Does the leader have support from the district to move ahead? Can the leader look at an approach that is not "one size fits all." What types of staff development might come from knowing where the staff currently is and what needs they have? I believe the more you can engage people from the start, being pro-active versus reactive is the right path to take.
>
> —Program Coordinator–Elementary ESL

> But really Frank, Betsy, and Vu are all victims of the shoddy policies of their school district. When it comes to the success of our children, no expense should be spared, for they truly are our future. If one can't get the support of their school administrators, then it is our job as teachers to find out a way to help children like Vu on our own.
>
> —Second Year Teacher

> This school would function much better, and Frank and Betty would feel much less stressed and indecisive if the protocol for ESL students was more spelled out for them and decided upon by the whole staff or district. There are no decisions that should be made on an individual basis in regards to how a teacher feels about a student. Individual factors should be included in a wider set of data collected about the student before decisions like moving students in and out of ESL are made.
>
> —Master's Candidate

Understanding Second Language Development:
Students Need ESL Instruction

Frank's actions reflect his current understandings of how students learn best. He, like most mainstream teachers, has not received any preparation that could help him respond to the needs of second language learners. As described in the case, many of Frank's colleagues felt that just being immersed in English all day long should be sufficient. Most respondents, however, called for Frank to put Vu back in ESL where the teacher would build on her understanding of second language development to organize instruction. Those experienced in teaching second language learners maintain that it is necessary for students to be in settings where teachers are focused on making instruction comprehensible.

> Frank was well prepared to teach the "average" student. . . . But his methods of instruction are not effective for English language learners. In fact, Frank approached Vu's language acquisition process as if Vu were in need of REMEDIATION. Frank places him in the lowest reading group and worked with him tutorial style. Vu needed MEDIATION between concepts in content areas and the English used to dialogue about and construct meaning with these concepts.
>
> —Third Grade Teacher

> This case represents what is reality for the majority of ESL students and their regular classroom teachers. Teachers may be extraordinary in their content area, but if they lack the training necessary to implement ESL strategies their teaching methods will fall short of effectively preparing lessons and activities that will meet the needs of their students. As is the case with Frank, he felt that he was doing all that was necessary and that his classroom was adapted to meet the learning styles of all students. It may very well have been set up that way, but Vu was not suffering from instruction that did not meet his learning style, but rather from his inability to understand instruction in a second language.
>
> —Elementary Teacher

> Frank is an effective mediator between concepts and culturally normative learners. He can bank on a certain amount of shared experiences that his students come to school with. Unfortunately, Frank can not bank on Vu's shared experiences while trying to mediate content area concepts because communication must also be mediated to insure Vu's progress.
>
> —Third Grade Teacher

Frank has not been prepared to teach the students he is being asked to educate. He is not being provided the skills he needs to do a good job for these students. Perhaps we could blame him for not taking more initiative to learn about [second language acquisition] and ESL instruction, but with the already heavy workload of teachers, even this is hard to do. I'd like to believe that as a teacher I will never allow a fate such as Vu's befall any of my students. I guess what scares me most is that despite MY best intentions, and despite the education I have received, and will continue to expand upon as a teacher, I may some day find that I too have failed my students.

—Master's Program Student

To many, Frank's actions indicate that he did not understand the distinction between surface oral fluency and academic proficiency. This leads many teachers to overestimate students' proficiency based on their initial successes at communicating around familiar topics.

Frank doesn't understand the developmental hierarchy of second language acquisition. L2 students first develop Basic Interpersonal Communicative skills (BICS), allowing them to communicate socially and perform basic tasks, and then later develop CALP, Cognitive Academic Language Proficiency, which gives them the language to express higher order thinking and academic concepts. When Vu demonstrates proficiency in BICS, Frank incorrectly assesses his readiness to transition full time back into the classroom. Back in the classroom, Vu flounders because he does not have the vocabulary for the academic concepts. Without the content support from ESL, Vu loses academic ground in the classroom.

—Elementary Teacher

I think that Betsy succumbed to some very typical pressures from teachers who don't understand second language learners, and allowed Vu to be taken out of ESL too early. Many people still believe that ESL is only for basic oral language development and want to move kids out when the student "speaks" English. This ignores the part of the language competence and takes many more years. Many well meaning teachers also push for getting kids into mainstream situations as soon as they are orally proficient so that the students don't feel "different." While this is a lofty goal, the second language student still feels different because he or she knows that they can't compete academically in the environment.

—District Central Office Secondary Program Coordinator

Children and adults alike cannot be expected to acquire proficiency in English within a one to two year period. Repeatedly, data indicates that the time needed for an individual to become proficient in a second language takes five to seven years. We need to allow our students to achieve success, build a foundation of knowledge, and strengthen the skills in their primary language, so that English acquisition can more readily transfer from the first language to the second. Yet as a society, we have neither the resources nor the inclination to make appropriate changes.

—Master's Candidate

There are conflicting views over when a student should receive special services and whether immersion in an all-English classroom is preferable to pull-out instruction focused on ESL. Disagreements arise over the best way to deliver ESL services with much of the tension focused on whether a pullout model helps or merely disrupts their instructional program.

I have watched teachers get frustrated with their ESL students. For an hour a day these children are pulled from the classroom for special instruction. They miss math, reading, history, or language arts. Many times they come back to class in the middle of a lesson and are lost. Because they do not know what is going on, they cause disruptions and keep others from learning. The teachers I have spoken to about this issue feel that their ESL students don't care about school or are lazy. They blame the child much like Frank does toward the end of this piece. I feel it is a combination of the child, the teachers, and the system that cause ESL students to withdraw and become behavior problems.

—Elementary Teacher

The appropriate time for Vu to be in ESL with Betsy would be during Frank's language arts period. It seems obvious that the remedial reading group with native language students was not an appropriate place for Vu. He is not a native language learner struggling with reading in his first language. His issues have to deal with English being his second language. His interest in figuring out words in text does not mean that he is ready to read in his second language independently.

—Second Grade Teacher–English component
of a dual immersion bilingual program

Betsy's initial focus with Vu relied heavily on oral language development—skills that would be essential for Vu to have in order to succeed. In addition, these skills would eventually help Vu to transfer his linguistic understanding over to those necessary for reading and decoding. However, in

the meantime, he is missing out on direct reading instruction, which will
only serve to frustrate him in the long run.

—Master's Candidate

It is my opinion that Vu needs the focused language instruction that ESL
classes provide. I don't believe that all children can successfully master a new
language vicariously. It is not enough for them to simply hear the language,
they must also practice the language, preferably in a non-threatening environment. In the classroom, Vu is forced to compete with children who have spent
their entire lives speaking and hearing English. I don't believe that this is an
environment that is as conducive to risk-taking as an ESL class, in which all
of the children are at a similar level linguistically. I think that Vu would benefit from the comfort and support of the ESL class. It would give him an opportunity to take the risks necessary for him to succeed in learning English. I
think that for this reason, Frank should admit that although he had Vu's best
interest in mind, he might not have made the right decision by pulling Vu out
of ESL class. Franks should swallow his pride and allow Betsy to do what she
was trained to do, teach English as a second language.

—Elementary Teacher

One of the troubling aspects about this case is the school-wide ignorance
about the needs of students like Vu. Betsy appears to be one of the only
teachers who knows anything about second language acquisition and the
school is taking no steps to see that the staff gains this much needed information. It frightens me that this type of situation actually occurs in schools
today, but I realize that it does. It makes me feel sick that children are being
denied a proper education, and being made to suffer, because of the ignorance about the needs of second language learners. It is also frustrating that
there is really no one to blame. It would be much easier if I could point to
Frank's maliciousness, and his wanton disregard for his duty as a teacher as
the cause of Vu's terrible situation. I would like to harangue the ESL
teacher for giving in to the whims of the classroom teacher. Unfortunately,
the actions they took are all too understandable.

—Prospective Teacher

All Teachers Should Understand
Second-Language Acquisition

Other readers maintained that with the increasing numbers of students
who speak English as a second language, all teachers need skills and strategies for working with this population. This begins with an understanding

of second language acquisition and the learning of particular instructional techniques. It extends to a commitment not only to utilize appropriate strategies, but to support each teacher's role in a student's overall program.

> The discussions between Betsy and Frank touched on the need for ALL teachers to receive training in ESL methodologies, and sadly, the potential resentment, and lack of willingness to participate from many staff members. This too represents a disappointing reality: the disconnect between classroom teachers and specialists who many times operate their classrooms as separate domains, rather than interconnected supports for the students.
>
> —Master's Candidate

> The ESL methods of instruction that Betsy mentioned to Frank were not just "good ideas" that might be helpful. ESL methods for language acquisition and concept development are ESSENTIAL pedagogy for English language learners if these students are to be successful in school.
>
> —Fourth Grade Teacher

> The entire school community must commit to consistently sending second language students to their daily instruction times, and teachers must realize that language development needs cannot be addressed solely on a one hour a day pullout basis. The entire school day must provide these students with support in the language acquisition process, as well as content reinforcement. Classroom teachers must share the responsibility for these students with ESL teachers; they must also insist that ESL students attend their pullout instruction times instead of resenting the schedule disruption or refusing to send students altogether. Additionally, the entire staff must agree to work together to coordinate the instruction offered in the ESL classroom and that of the regular classrooms. Instead of not "finding the time" this staff must "make the time" to coordinate with the ESL teacher. All teachers must learn ESL techniques in order to support students in their English acquisition, reinforcing vocabulary and concept development and facilitating their literacy in all areas, content areas as well as Language Arts.
>
> —Graduate Student

> The entire staff needs to be supported in learning more about first and second language acquisition and how to work with second language learners in the mainstream setting. Although some will be resistant, the receptive teachers should not be denied access to the information because of a few naysayers. There are people resistant to ANY changes but you reach the

teachers who are ready to be reached and looking for new answers. One way to approach this is to have a teacher study group, which is optional for the people who are ready to really take off on this topic. Mentor teachers who have the experience to share are ideal, but frequently not enough are available. Educational leadership would be an important aspect here—the district and school leaders need to make teaching second language learners as important as any other skills. This is part of the future of U.S. public schools, if current demographic trends continue.

—District Central Office Secondary Program Coordinator

By reflecting on his experience with Vu, Frank should realize several things. He does need special training to effectively teach students like Vu. Frank seemed to think that his enthusiasm would be enough, but it's not. Neither is the handful of conversations he had with Betsy, the ESL teacher. Frank and the other teachers at his school need to take classes in order to better understand second language acquisition and how it affects students in their classrooms like Vu. Furthermore, ESL is necessary and important for longer than six months. It may seem like an intrusion, but with classroom coordination it could be lessened.

—Graduate Student

It is a mistake to think that ESL programs are not necessary because the student will learn English anyway. For students in this situation, the regular school day can be a long and confusing experience. Often, the only time they receive any meaningful instruction is when they are in their ESL classrooms.

—Elementary Teacher

Many individuals felt that Betsy's demonstration in Spanish was a very effective strategy to sensitize them to the frustration and embarrassment their ESL students often suffer.

Betsy was wise to give Frank an example by putting him in the student's place. Unless we know how it feels, it is hard for us to understand, relate, and help these students. Such a thing happened to me when I was in all Spanish speaking kindergarten. Just like Frank, I had to "tune out" a lot of what was going on around me. The situation became frustrating and confusing, since I was only able to understand a small percentage of what was going on. It is important to know what our non-English speaking students are experiencing.

—Elementary Teacher

Reconnect With Vu

A common view was that Frank should reach out directly to Vu to try and get his point of view and reestablish the trust that had been lost. In addition, respondents felt that in each setting, Vu was simply responding to expectations put on him.

> Vu probably only sees what he is incapable of doing, not the successes he has made.
>
> —Teacher working on ESL endorsement

> Frank has earned Vu's distrust. The teachers need to explain to Vu that they made a mistake and seek his ideas as to how things could be put right again. Hopefully, they will all come to an agreement to put Vu back in ESL. It would also be helpful for Frank to get some instruction in using sheltering techniques in his classroom so Vu can be more successful during the time that he is with Frank. It could also be useful to find some specific responsibilities for Vu (hopefully his choice) that would help him feel valuable in Frank's classroom or in the school at large. The teachers need to help him get his self-confidence back.
>
> —Middle School ESL Teacher

> Not only does Frank need to examine his teaching practices with Vu, but he also needs to consider how his total learning environment in his classroom may affect Vu and other special learners that he has in class. I get the feeling from the case study that Frank is confident that his classroom environment will help all of his students to succeed. . . . I believe that if Frank seriously investigates the environment he has created, he will then find that other students in the class might also learn better in a slightly different environment. Frank's classroom may be very effective for more "traditional" learners, but has he taken individual differences into account?
>
> —Graduate Student

> The enthusiasm that Frank and Vu have is contagious in the beginning and many classmates are willing to help Vu. However, as time progresses Vu becomes more and more frustrated because he does not understand everything that is going on in class. Frank's expectations of Vu become blurred and he becomes frustrated as well. Other students in the classroom are no longer willing to help Vu. This is due primarily to the concept of teacher expectation. Often, a teacher's high expectations of students can lead to a self-

fulfilling prophecy. The teacher shows high levels of positive expectation and the students come to believe that they are able to do well. There are many studies that support this such as Rosenthal and Jacobson's *Pygmalion in the Classroom* (2003). As Frank's enthusiasm lessened, Vu's enthusiasm to learn did as well. Frank needs to find a way to make the classroom a more meaningful experience for Vu and his peers.

—Upper Elementary Teacher

Build a Classroom Community

Students who receive ESL instruction usually receive it for just a short time each day. The rest of their day they are in the "regular" classroom where they often feel marginalized from the broader classroom community. A final theme in the reactions to this case was to encourage Frank to examine the entire classroom community. Respondents urged him to take steps that would involve students and teachers working together to build a safe environment and affirm children like Vu's cultural identity.

There is one last thing to mention. Classmates who were trying to help Vu may have been insensitive outside of the class or when Frank wasn't able to see. Vu appeared to change quickly and that would lead me to believe that his peers had something to do with that. Maybe they needed sensitivity training, how to help someone in a non-threatening manner. This has happened in my own class before. I had a girl before in my class and she was not able to even write her name. Everyone wanted to help her at first. Then, if I asked someone to work with her it, she seemed to be in the way. They would help her, but seemed to resent it. I had to have a few meetings with them [focused on affect] when she wasn't around. Then, I started to see progress with the way students treated her. It took many sessions, and help from the special education teacher as well to help run these affective classes for my students. It really did make a difference. With everyone's help students', teachers', and Frank's, Vu will regain their trust, but it takes a commitment from everyone!

—Elementary Teacher

[I suspect that] I am not providing the right kind of scaffolding for students who communicate less to access concepts and engage in construction of their own knowledge. If some students are constantly engaging with material more than other students and if the "other students" are constantly less engaged with material, I have to ask myself, "Am I satisfied with this classroom dynamic?" "Can I change my teaching practices to engage all students?"

—Teacher

In order to address the various problems that have come up in his own class regarding Vu, Frank must take actions that will show Vu that he cares about him and is there for him. If I were in Frank's position, I would start by admitting to Vu that I had made a mistake and ask him for his forgiveness. This may be hard thing for many teachers to do, but I think it is important to let students know that you are human and make mistakes just like everyone else. It is also important to show your students that you are able to admit your mistakes and learn from them, as you expect your students to do. In addition, by apologizing to Vu, Frank will let Vu know that he cares about his well being and is trying to do what is best for him.

—Graduate Student

READER REACTIONS TO
"THE CYCLE: FRANK AND VU"

SUMMARY AND ADDITIONAL QUESTIONS

Teachers are more likely than not to begin their careers with little information about linguistic diversity. Usually the focus of their preparation has
been on strategies and approaches that are designed for the needs of monolingual English speakers. Until they have to actually teach second language learners, they may be unaware of the special challenges of providing appropriate instruction to this population. What happened to Frank
happens to many teachers. One day, with little or no warning, children
who do not speak English arrive in their classroom and it is up to them to
figure out what to do.

Seemingly the logical first step is to try to fit the new students into the
existing routine. In trying to meet any new challenge most people will rely
on what has worked for them in the past to determine what to do in the future. If their native English speakers have been progressing well, they will
likely continue to teach the way they have been teaching all along. If the
second language learners do not succeed, it easy to think the students are
not doing their part to learn by not responding to instruction. It takes a
while to realize that, in fact, it may be the instruction that is not responsive
to the needs of the students. Given a limited knowledge base and experience with second language learners it is understandable why some teachers might blame the student for failing to thrive despite their best efforts.
This can lead to frustration on many levels. When teachers eventually recognize that their approaches need to change, as good teachers always will,
they will need to ask for help. This can conflict with the sense of autonomy
that teachers often feel when they working with one group of students for
whom they are completely responsible all day. It is not part of most teachers' socialization to share responsibility for students or to ask their peers
for assistance. They may believe that to ask for help makes them appear
less than competent. Well meaning teachers can easily find themselves in
Frank's situation. As you think further about the implications of this case,
the following questions are important to consider.

- What are the benefits and drawbacks of providing specialized services to small groups of students outside the grade level classroom?
  How can the challenges be overcome?
- How can teachers learn to see students' behaviors as an interaction
  between their methods and the lives and stresses of the students?

- How can teachers become aware that their instruction might be the problem?
- How can teachers become more confident about seeking help and support?
- What should teachers do when they feel they are more informed than the building leadership about a particular area of instruction or group of students?
- How do teachers' expectations for students affect their behavior? How are these expectations shaped in relation to students' cultural and linguistic background?

INTRODUCTION TO CASE 2

When teachers and students have similar cultural backgrounds, their shared cultural understandings promote communication and can provide comfortable interactions. When teachers' backgrounds differ greatly from those of their students, these cultural differences can cause misunderstandings and miscommunication. This is compounded when teachers lack awareness about students' lives before coming to the United States, and have limited knowledge regarding the circumstances in which the students currently live.

This is important because as students move from home to school the differing expectations and norms in each setting may reveal varying aspects of their competence, personality, and self-concept. This is especially true for students whose linguistic and cultural backgrounds differ from those of the dominant population in the school. At home, they may rely on a completely different set of skills and assets, untapped, and unseen at school. Because there are both social skills and/or problem solving abilities around non-academic topics, students who do not speak English are often prevented from effectively utilizing all of their cognitive and social skills in school. When these mismatches occur, as they do frequently these students find themselves in settings that restrict their potential contributions causing many of them to shut down.

In this case, you will meet Marisa, a junior high student and one of her teachers, Jane. The case describes how one teacher makes the effort to learn about a student who concerns her. It reveals some of the many ways that misjudgments of students can occur when teachers lack information regarding students and their family life. It also presents information that sheds a different light on the common perception that parents from certain cultural backgrounds don't care about academic achievement and can't or won't help their children succeed in school.

Issues raised in this case include: What is known about the students we teach? Whose responsibility is it to provide a coherent educational program for students? What difference can one teacher make? How can teachers better build on students' strengths to enhance academic learning? What are possible consequences of the distance between teachers and the communities they serve?

CASE 2: "MARISA'S PROSPECTS"

Jane had taught at Green Junior High School for 4 years. Lately she has been very concerned about the progress of one of her students, a ninth grader named Marisa. Marisa is very quiet and seems to have few friends. She is a hard-working student but she often struggles with ninth grade reading selections. Although she is quite good at talking about stories and other narratives she has read, she seems to miss the main point of the expository text found in the social studies and science books. Marisa's grades from elementary school were average and above and Jane has thought of Marisa as an intelligent and capable student, but Jane is beginning to question whether she has overestimated Marisa's abilities. Marisa seems to be missing the obvious, like in the report she did on life cycles where the main point of the assignment was to describe how different animals have life cycles that are adapted to their environment. Although Marisa was able to describe each part of the life cycle, she was not able to synthesize the information regarding adaptations, one of the big ideas focused on in this unit.

Another thing that is bothering Jane is that lately Marisa's behavior has taken a turn for the worse. She is becoming somewhat moody and has trouble getting along with the other students and in cooperative group activities. Jane wishes she had an explanation. When she hears other teachers talking about problems of Latino students, their explanation is that their families don't help with class work and don't really value education. They say these parents aren't really interested in their children's progress. They contend that this limits their ability to learn and explains their lack of motivation. Jane has noticed that it is really hard to get homework back from some students, and that there are rarely any Latino parents who volunteer at school or attend back to school night. However, these explanations seem too simplistic to Jane. Even if it were true that Marisa's parents didn't care about her education, Marisa has, up to now, been working hard on her schoolwork. Jane is sure that Marisa has a lot of potential and she doesn't want to lose her. She is worried about the slide in her behavior and academics she is beginning to see develop. She knows Marisa is approaching an age when many students drop out and Jane wants to do something to prevent this if she can.

Marisa has sometimes mentioned how much she liked her sixth grade teacher, Carolyn, at Eagle Elementary school. Jane decides to call Carolyn to check on whether she has overestimated Marisa's abilities, and to see what insights and advice her former teacher might offer.

Carolyn, who has taught at Eagle for 8 years, is happy to hear from Jane. In her experience, this is the first time anyone from the junior high school has ever called. She teaches many Latino students at Eagle and has often wondered how they do when they move on to junior high. She has worked closely with the families in her community and has developed a strong level of respect for the hardship many of the families are experiencing. Carolyn is impressed that a junior high school teacher would take the time to get more information about an individual student's background.

Carolyn listens as Jane relates her concerns about Marisa. Jane explains how she had seen a great deal of potential in Marisa, but now worries that she might be wrong. She asks what Carolyn had observed about Marisa as a student. She expresses concern that she has never seen Marisa's parents at school and that they do not return her calls. She tells Carolyn that she hates to think they don't care, but that seems to be the general consensus of the teachers she has talked to at her school. She asks if Carolyn thinks that the lack of response from Marisa's parents means that there is little hope that Marisa can be successful in school.

First Carolyn confirms that Marisa is a very hardworking and bright girl. She explains to Jane that Marisa has only been in the United States since the fifth grade. Although she is very fluent in English in social situations, she still needs a good deal of support in English language development. Carolyn tells Jane that by listening closely to how Marisa talks, she will get many clues to where support is needed. For example, she asks Jane if she has noticed that Marisa will often use a round-about way to explain what she means rather than the precise word, for example, "all the people around" instead of "the crowd," or "the thing that closes the door" instead of the latch. She explains that it is not that Marisa is not smart enough to understand academic concepts, but rather that her lack of familiarity with English vocabulary often makes it difficult for her to understand all of the information she needs in order to answer questions in greater depth.

Jane asks if she can share a sample of Marisa's written work with Carolyn over the telephone. As Jane reads aloud the passage that Marisa has written, she realizes that she sounds just like Marisa does when she talks. It dawns on Jane that many of the errors in Marisa's writing reflect her oral pronunciation and probably gaps in her English language development. Carolyn agrees. She tells Jane that she noticed the same thing as the material became harder and more abstract (e.g., when they began to study U.S. history and the meaning of concepts such as democracy and individual rights). She needed to teach in ways that would help Marisa gain a better understanding of the material they were covering. Carolyn describes the special lessons she planned to demonstrate what the words meant in order to help Marisa and several other second language learners better understand. She stresses the importance of the conversations she had with them in a small group so that they would get experience in expressing their ideas about the abstract concepts. If they didn't know the words they needed she would model and have students practice using them and saying them out loud. Interestingly enough when she started focusing on giving the second language learners of English in her class a better understanding of the more complicated concepts, her lessons helped all of the students in the class to understand the ideas better. She said she hadn't realized how many of the native speakers were also missing the point.

Carolyn strongly encourages Jane to visit Marisa's home. She tells her that Marisa's mother works all day but even so, she always used to spend several hours each evening helping Marisa with her schoolwork. She says that Marisa's parents are very proud of her and have high hopes for her future.

Jane decides to take her colleague's advice and visit Marisa's family. Trying to set up a time to visit when both of Marisa's parents can be there is difficult. It seems that when one parent comes home, the other leaves for work. After several attempts, a day is found that works for all of them.

As Jane drives up to Marisa's house she sees a group of neighborhood children organized into what seems to be a highly competitive game of soccer. As she watches she is surprised to see that Marisa is a leader in the group, yelling out commands and urging one of the teams forward. Marisa is animated, authoritative, and very expressive. What surprises Jane even more is that all of the kids, including Marisa, are speaking only Spanish. Because Marisa always speaks English at school, Jane just assumed that she preferred English and that it was her dominant language. She had never heard Marisa speak Spanish at school and does not think of her as a bilingual student. She wonders if there are other students like Marisa who only speak English at school but use Spanish at home. As Jane enters the house she is also surprised to see a little bookcase in the corner of the living room with collection of well-worn books, magazines and newspapers in both Spanish and English. She wonders why she is surprised.

Marisa's parents greet Jane warmly but are apprehensive in part because their English fluency is limited. No teacher has ever visited at home before and they are afraid there is bad news. Jane begins by explaining that she wants to share with parents some of the activities her students do. As Marisa's parents become more comfortable she begins to broach the subject that prompted her visit. At that moment Marisa slips quietly into the room. Having noticed the car in front of her house she has come to investigate. Her mother motions for her to join them on the couch.

Jane begins to explain her concerns about Marisa. She tells Marisa's parents about the potential she sees in Marisa, but that recently her behavior has begun to change. She is not sure what is happening but wants to know if they can help her understand Marisa's change and suggest ways in which Jane can help her to get back on the right track.

Marisa's mother turns to Marisa and quickly asks her in Spanish what is going on with her. An animated conversation ensues between Marisa and her parents. When they have finished Marisa's mother explains that Marisa doesn't understand a lot of what is going on at school, but is afraid to say so. According to her mother, Marisa thinks the schoolwork has gotten much more difficult to understand and there is no one there who helps students when they do not understand the materials.

Last year, she explains, there was a teacher who had spent special time with bilingual students to help them understand what they were studying. She tells Jane that they don't know why that person isn't there this year, but having lost her help, Marisa has tried a new strategy in her studies. Every night she translates the material into Spanish. Then she and her mother talk about what they think it means and she completes the assignment in Spanish. Then Marisa uses the Spanish–English dictionary they have bought her to translate all of her work back into English again. As Jane listens she realizes that this may explain why papers she gets from Marisa are stilted and sometimes contain the wrong vocabulary word for the context.

Marisa's mother says Marisa often works late into the night because all the translation takes a lot of time. She is often very tired in the morning. Her mother is worried because the material is also getting harder and less familiar for her and her husband. She is afraid that they will not be able to help their daughter much longer. Marisa's mother says they know they may not be providing enough help. She does want to support her daughter as much as possible and doesn't really know how else to keep involved with her schooling. Marisa's parents both appeal to Jane to find a way to help them support their daughter. They want Marisa to go to college and know she has the potential to be an excellent student. Marisa's dad adds, "Marisa is a very smart girl. We want her to have better than we have in life. We want her to continue her school."

Jane wasn't expecting to hear what Marisa's parents had to say. She remembers all the conversations in the lounge at school that constantly blame parents' lack of interest in their children's education for the students' academic difficulties. She can hardly remember a time when the talk was about what the school might do to get a better understanding of students' needs and how they might better support their learning.

Jane is frustrated with herself for not being more aware of her students' circumstances and so susceptible to accepting a point of view from other teachers that she has never really examined. She wonders why she so rarely puts herself in someone else's shoes, why she has never considered how it might feel to live in a home where the major language was let's say, German as her background would reflect. Going to school every day, she would have to shift not only ways of doing and thinking, but of ways of talking and presenting ideas. If there weren't special help available, how would she fare in that situation?

Jane recalls an experience during her teacher education program where a professor had given the class a paragraph to read on quantum physics. The professor had then asked the students to talk about the relationship of quarks and pions and how they were converted to antiquarks. Jane had been able to follow the reading on one level and even answer simple questions about the topic by going back and deducing the answer from the text. But, she remembers how lost she was in terms of any real understanding of what they had discussed. When she was asked how this information could be used to solve a problem in physics, she had no idea. And this lesson was in English! She also recalls her own experience trying to learn German and the frustration of trying to get her point across in German to a German exchange student. She could certainly understand how Marisa might struggle with particular topics.

At this point in the conversation Marisa blurts out that she has tried to work harder and harder but the work is getting too difficult. Her face reveals the intensity of the frustration she is feeling. She says there are many things she is not familiar with in her classes, she finds it difficult to ask teachers for help, and when they do respond to her, it is often so quickly that she doesn't catch all the words. She is far too embarrassed to ask again and just pretends to have understood. "I get very angry when I work so hard and I still do not understand like other students," Marisa tells her. "I know that if the teachers would give me more time to think about it and give examples I could do much better."

On her way home Jane reflects on what Marisa and students like her face every day. They are working in two linguistic worlds and are asked to compete with monolingual English speakers without additional English language support. They are often considered less able. She also thinks about the richness of language and the support that Marisa has all around her. The picture of Marisa, leading the soccer team, flashes through her mind. She wonders, again, how many other students at Green are having the same struggles and why she and other teachers don't seem to understand. It strikes her that living in a world with two languages means living a much more complex environment than Jane is accustomed to. She is expecting Marisa, whose world includes two languages, to be as proficient in English in 4 years as her other students were in only one language in 13 years.

Jane has so many doubts and so many questions. She knows that there are many, many students like Marisa. How is she going to help them be successful? She only has Marisa for one period a day, and given the lack of awareness she has observed in other teachers she is sure not much is being done to help Marisa with regard to language development in her other classes. How much could really be done in only one hour per day?

When she sits back and thinks about the complexity of the situation it seems daunting. The teachers at Green Junior High School rarely talk about language issues except to complain about the level or student skills and it has never been a topic of discussion at staff meetings. Carolyn told her that she was the first junior high school teacher who had ever called her to learn more about the students that fed into their school. This seemed to be a school-wide problem. How could she help other teachers to understand the dilemma that second language learners face at Green? How could she ever hope to make a difference? What would it mean if she actually got involved in changing the school?

The worst thing is, she really doesn't know what to do. Is there really a way she could help? How much time will it take her to find out and anyway wouldn't Marisa be moving on to high school next year? Jane is sure she doesn't have time for more classes or for learning new techniques. She is already working hard to help her students. How can she take on any more responsibility? Can she really afford to get this involved in the education of one student? On the other hand, if she learned more about how to help Marisa she could probably become more effective in meeting the needs of other students, as well. Where should she start or, then again, should she?

Jane decides to call a close friend who was in her teacher preparation program for help in deciding what to do. If it were you, what advice would you give to Jane? Is it up to her to do something? If so, what?

READER REACTIONS TO
MARISA AND JANE'S SITUATION

REACTIONS TO "MARISA'S PROSPECTS"

The responses to this case echo several of the themes presented in the previous case, that individuals must act, seek information, and utilize appropriate instructional strategies. What is unique to this case is the attention focused on home–school relationships. Responses address the perceptions that teachers often hold of non-English speaking parents and the disconnection between students' lives at home and at school.

Change Is Difficult to Experience

Again and again, respondents to this case addressed the need for schools to change in the face of current demographic trends. A subtext to this was that individual teachers must step up and be the catalyst when they know that something is wrong, even if they don't know exactly what to do and have difficulty facing all of the varied tasks.

> In answer to the question, "How could she take on any more responsibility?" The answer is "When you're a teacher your responsibility is to help all children be successful, not just the ones that are easy for you."
> —Fifth Grade Teacher

> One of the questions posed towards the end of the case study is, "How much time would it take her to find out, and anyway wouldn't Marisa be gone to high school next year?" Unfortunately, I feel that this is an attitude that is taken far too often by far too many people: educators, politicians, etc. Marisa may be moving on next year, but children in her same situation will continue to move through the school system. In addition, if the demographics of that school are changing, they are most likely changing district-wide. Teaching English language learners is not going to be any easier if the district and individual schools don't figure out a way to meet their needs.
> —Bilingual Teacher–English component

> Reading this case study reminded me that the challenge of educating second language learners is truly complex and multidimensional, deeply rooted in socio-cultural, political and pedagogical contexts. When teachers first realize why many language minority students are having "learning difficulties" and "behavior problems," they also realize the enormous and often overwhelming efforts required for creating change. It is easy to blame the family and home environment for the failure of these children. However, as more

teachers like Jane question "why" and explore the deeper issues involved, the more change will begin to unfold.

—Elementary Teacher

Jane should try to dispel some of the misguided perceptions that exist within the school. The easiest way to do this is to focus on Marisa and other students like her. Jane may not be able to change the attitudes of other teachers within the school, but she can work to create her own success that others can emulate. Educating other teachers about her experience, and informing them of successful teaching strategies will keep the lines of communication open and create an environment where teachers can work together for the benefit of all students.

—Graduate Student

It seems to me that people in the school who are like Jane are a rare find, and this is depressing. Their team needs to open their eyes and see that the responsibility for these children is partly theirs. Jane is on the right track, but unfortunately, with little support from others, will probably give up before she reaches a solution. It seems to me that her school and colleagues need a lot of education on this matter, and need to start the wheel of change, because now, something is not working.

—Elementary Bilingual Teacher

There is only so much time in a day and so much a teacher can do. Where does a single person begin? When does a teacher say they have to attend to their own family? There are so many meetings and after school obligations that somehow this should be a point to be brought up at these meetings, instead of being left to talk in the lounge. It is so much more complex and too often teachers are speaking out of generalizations instead of individual students.

—Teacher

I think Jane has to pace herself because if she doesn't she might burn out, which happens to a lot of teachers, especially teachers of minority students. (It happened to me).

—Doctoral Student

I have a great deal of respect for this teacher. She has gone above and beyond what is expected of a teacher, she has tried to find an underlying problem of one of her students. While she knew that the student was smart, she also knew she was struggling at her schoolwork. This teacher could have just let the student struggle and get farther behind as many busy teachers will do, but she took time out of her busy day to find an answer. This reading made me feel good about the extra things I do for my students that other teachers tell me isn't part of my job.

—Teacher

Readers spoke to the negative consequences of the lack of communication and the failure to share information about students across levels within a school district and among various personnel in the same school. Concerns were expressed about how little secondary teachers usually know about their students. Many called for greater, and more structured, communication across levels.

It is appalling to me that in the transition from one level to the next within the same school district, the appropriate information is not passed on in order to ease a child into a new system.

—Prospective Teacher

I, too, wish there were contact between the elementary and the middle school. We have our students for six hours every day, and they only get them for an hour each day. For this reason we know an awful lot about our students and how they work or don't work, and we would like to share this information so our students can continue to be successful.

—Fifth Grade Teacher

Jane shows herself to be quite an open individual, by calling the elementary to see how Marisa functioned in that setting. It would be useful for the school district to set up some kind of transition conferences or other method for the teachers to actually share information about students when they move from one school to another.

—Secondary Second Language Program Coordinator

What Should Jane Do?

Respondents were clear that Jane should act on what she has discovered about Marisa and her family and use this knowledge to improve her instruction. As for the exact steps Jane should take, the opinions varied, especially about where to start. Should she begin with herself, approach other staff members or go directly to the administration with her concerns? Many advised her to seek help from the principal, as soon as possible. No matter where Jane begins, readers caution her to start slowly, find allies, and above all, try to avoid burnout.

Jane could help Marisa in a variety of ways. For instance, she could work on modifying her lessons in order for Marisa to receive the greatest benefit (regarding language learning/acquisition and concept development). She could also discuss the issue with the building's administrators and request professional development workshops that addressed the needs of their ESL population.

—Doctoral Student

Jane asks where she might start to take on responsibility for more consciously educating Marisa and students like her. First, she must decide in what way she is willing to defend her position which places the responsibility of educating the children on the teachers and administration [and not just] on the children. Emboldened, she may try to bring the faculty along with her on her educational journey. I would suggest, however, that she start quietly, within her own classroom, making subtle changes that, with time, will prove the efficacy of her approaches.

—Prospective Teacher

Often when teachers are faced with situations such as Jane's, we incorrectly perceive the need to work harder at what we are doing instead of working smarter. While Jane already had taken steps to work smarter, she failed to recognize them. These steps included forming a network of support with more successful, experienced teachers of second language learners, creating and maintaining a home–school connection, and consulting with students on a regular basis as an integral part of assessment practices.

—Literacy Coach

This teacher can't really change the teachers' attitudes. She needs to educate the other teachers in her school about the problems the second language learners face on a daily basis. When she hears other teachers talk about how they feel about these learners, she needs to speak up for them. Often people make up their minds about others without all the facts. These teachers need to see their classrooms from the eyes of the students. Look to see how their attitudes and teaching styles affect their students.

—Graduate Student

In Jane's mind, the problem is school wide, thus, Jane really does need to share her frustrations and concerns immediately with the building leader and bring to the discussion how she knows that there are other students also not being as successful as they are capable of becoming.

—Elementary ESL Program Coordinator

I think that the first action that Jane should take is to discuss the problem with her school's principal. By doing so, she would not only be bringing an important issue to the principal's attention that he/she may not have thought of before, but she would also no longer be dealing with the problem alone. After the principal had been contacted he/she may set in motion an evaluation of the school's effectiveness with educating Limited English Proficient students. This evaluation process would then provide a stepping stone for improving the school's instruction of second language learners.

—Prospective Teacher

I am happy to hear that a teacher discovered Marisa's potential and is going to do her best to not let her "fall through the cracks." Jane needs to confront her principal and let her know Marisa's background as well as the information she gathered at the home visit. As the case states, there are more children than Marisa who need some English reinforcement and instruction. While speaking to the principal, Jane needs to ask what school district resources are available to her. What do other schools in the district do for ESL students? Is there a school Jane can observe to learn how to reinforce the English language and teach new concepts in English as well?

—Teacher

Jane might consider bringing the topic up at a staff meeting so that all of the teachers in the school would hear her concerns. She might also try to persuade the principal or the committee in charge of scheduling inservices to schedule an upcoming teacher workshop that would address the needs of second language learners. By doing so, she would help bring the topic of meeting LEP students' needs to the attention of the school's staff. In addition, a workshop would also help introduce them all, including Jane, to some of the strategies for improving their instruction of LEP students. Because inservices are already required of teachers, these sessions would not present added work for the staff. If Jane could arrange this type of staff development, she might feel better armed to help students like Marisa and she would not feel so alone in her struggle with this topic. Even if she just brings the problem to the attention of the school's staff, Jane has taken an important step toward improving the situation.

—Prospective Teacher

Why Aren't Students Progressing Faster?
Social Versus Academic Competence

Jane is frustrated by the seemingly slow academic progress of students like Marisa. Often teachers are disappointed that students don't rise to the expectations they have developed based on students' oral fluency in English. What many fail to realize is that surface oral proficiency does not equate to academic proficiency. To be academically successful students must do much more than express themselves around familiar topics. They must also be able to comprehend complex text structures and express complicated ideas both orally and in writing. Unfortunately, at the secondary level, support for students' language development needs usually diminishes as the difficulty of the material increases.

Respondents felt that teachers need to develop an awareness of students' potential frustration as the content gets more demanding. They also have to realize that it is their responsibility to adapt their instruction to meet students' needs without "dumbing it down."

Jane found herself realizing that although her second language learners seemed to have very good social English, they lacked the academic language necessary to succeed in assignments that required problem solving, analysis, and critical thinking. I see this as a huge problem in the schools because our second language learners are not getting the advanced and ongoing ESL support they need. All too often, students are graduated from ESL when their social English is acceptable and they are able to "get by." In my experience the reason for this is that ESL services are generally very limited and, therefore, the most critical students (usually those who have most recently arrived from a foreign country and speak no English) are given priority. While recent arrivals obviously need ESL support, when we graduate students from ESL programs without giving them the skills they need to survive in an academic setting, we are setting them up for failure.
—Third Year Teacher

Students who experience academic success in a second language (English) during their elementary years often suffer extreme frustration when the content becomes more academic and difficult in the upper grades. Teachers need to be conscious of this transition to better serve second language learners of English. Not realizing that there are language issues at play, teachers are often unsuccessful at aiding students to reach their full potential. Even if students are no longer receiving ESL services, teachers need to be aware of the language diversity that exists within their classrooms.
—Prospective Teacher

Jane's discussion with Marisa's previous teacher brought up some critical issues often overlooked. These issues include that second language learners often lack sufficient vocabulary or language constructs to represent their learnings in English because they were not explicitly taught to them. Second language learners (along with many other students) lack an understanding of the formal constraints of written language as compared to oral language use, again because too often they are not explicitly taught. And second language learners need multiple opportunities over time to practice integrating and using modeled vocabulary and language constructs.

—Literacy Coach

The Need for Self-Reflection

Many respondents suggested that teachers should step back and examine their own instructional practice before blaming students, or their home environments, for their academic difficulties.

I criticize myself for the times that I have failed to remember the old adage: walk a mile in someone else's shoes. It is far too easy to place blame on an external source such as the student or the family, or even the culture, rather than step back and investigate the effectiveness of our own teaching strategies. Does my instructional program meet the needs of this individual learner? Such a simple question. I think that I might enlarge it, laminate it, and hang it in my classroom as a permanent reminder that I am a critical player in this scenario, as well.

—Master's Candidate

I have seen students, much like Marisa, who become frustrated with what is going on in class and have a hard time relating their frustrations with the teacher and their peers. One of the things that I find very important in helping these students is reflecting on what I am doing as a teacher to help these students.

—Elementary Teacher

School communities need to realize that students' problems are directly related to the lack of comprehensible input provided in the classrooms; confounded by the fact that these children speak an entirely different language at home. I am reminded of the ignorant school community in which I work. There is little understanding by the staff of my school of the deeper issues involved in educating our language minority students. As I continue in my

Master's program, I learn more about how detrimental some of our school's teaching practices are. We are an English-only school and yet we have over one-third of our students coming to school speaking a language other than English. In our staff meetings, there is plenty of discussion about parents who don't show up for conferences, who don't volunteer, or who don't care. And there are plenty of negative inferences about the children who do not speak English in our school. Never have I heard any discussion about techniques that can be used to teach these children. We have never had staff development or training to discuss or learn new methods of instruction for English Language Learners.

—Elementary Teacher

Once teachers are aware that the nature of their instruction should change, they must then be equipped with particular strategies. These strategies are often collectively referred to as "sheltered instruction."

These suggestions were made by the elementary school teacher: taking time to demonstrate and explain concepts and vocabulary, modeling how to use these concepts and vocabulary in discourse, and scheduling time for English language learners to practice using their oral skills with one another and with native English speakers. These three components would benefit all students as instructional practices, but these components are essential for the success of English language learners.

—Intermediate Teacher

Jane should remain aware of who her ESL students are, and to group them together when appropriate. Small groups can be given special attention if they are struggling with a particular concept. Students can be encouraged to discuss the concept either amongst themselves, or with the teacher. Then the teacher can modify teaching strategies as appropriate within each group. Groups should be divided differently depending on the task. There may be situations where random grouping, or a more heterogeneous group, is appropriate. The most important thing is to give students a chance to talk about the material, ask questions, and receive clarification in a safe, environment, and to discover for themselves the meaning of the content. Again, these are just good teaching strategies that will benefit all students.

—Prospective Teacher

Often, however, teachers interpret "modification" to mean "watering down" the curriculum. Many teachers also lament that they don't have time to prepare extra lessons for the second language learners.

In effect, it is not that we have to water down the content to a demeaning level for students who are second language learners. Instead, the content should be adjusted to ensure that students get the same essential information, but are allocated more time and support to complete the assigned task.

—Master's Candidate

I think that the teacher can alter the instruction—not water it down—to help Marisa and also the strategies will help native speakers as well. I think that we often assume that in order to help second language learners, we have to set aside time to help them and work with them on a one-on-one basis. This in not true. Cooperative grouping and partner work can help develop the language skills when the teacher sets up the lesson appropriately. Of course, this takes a lot of effort, but the rewards outweigh the effort immensely.

—Upper Elementary Teacher

Everybody Gains

Many readers, particularly those who had tried these strategies in their classrooms, focused on the fact that the use of sheltering strategies was beneficial to all of their students.

Jane is "right on" in thinking that if she learns about how to help Marisa, she would in turn become more effective with other students. Her best bet might be to read the research on second language acquisition and blend it with what she knows to be true from the application standpoint before she shares with others.

—Elementary ESL Program Coordinator

I have found that when I modify my lessons in order to make them more understandable to my second language learners, I use more visual aids, more hands on activities and more interactive approaches. As a result, all of my students learn the material more thoroughly. This method of teaching is enjoyable, it is rewarding, and it is exhausting. It is really hard work. It requires detailed planning and preparation, which is very time consuming. I am not yet able to teach all of my lessons using all of these methods (I'm sure the teachers who do are incredibly dynamic and fabulous educators). However, I find that the more I teach, the better I become, and gradually these techniques filter into all aspects of my teaching. Due to the taxing nature of this method, I know that not all teachers will strive to teach like this. My hope though, is that by incorporating these methods into my teaching, I will give students a variety of tools and strategies to use in order to increase their understanding across content areas.

—Third Year Teacher

Carolyn talks about how the material becomes more difficult and more abstract. She needs to plan special lessons that demonstrate what these words mean in order to ensure understanding. The eye opener for Jane and for me in many of the classes I've taken and observed first hand, is that these strategies actually helped "All" of the students in the class to understand the ideas better, even the native speakers [of English]. This is very powerful and needs to be shared with all teachers. Everyone benefits.

—Third Grade Teacher

Role of Primary Language

This case also highlights the complicated relationship between students' learning in their first and second languages. Many believe that native language support is a temporary stop gap measure to help elementary age children make a quick transition to English. As demonstrated in this case, for older students the ideas and concepts they know in their first language can be consciously built on to help consolidate the conceptual understandings of their academic classes. Respondents suggest that by validating students' primary language in school, teachers can also begin to see parents as a resource to support students at home.

Still another step which needs to be taken and which was not readily in evidence was the need to begin focusing on what Marisa WAS capable of, and to begin building on her strengths and capabilities. This includes the recognition of Marisa's native language as a foundation for learning English.

—Literacy Coach

It seems like Marisa is getting very frustrated from working so hard and getting nowhere. The support of native language tutors in the content classrooms to help kids focus on concept development would be helpful. Marisa also needs to learn how to work smarter, not harder! She should not be doing so much translating—this takes endless amounts of time and doesn't allow her to focus on the concepts she is trying to learn. Since she has such active support with her homework from her Spanish-speaking parents, it could be helpful to find Spanish materials on the topics she is studying to read and discuss with her parents. It would also help if someone could help Marisa and her parents focus on concept development, instead of trying to get everything "done" without comprehension.

—Middle School ESL Teacher

The situation that Jane faced at Green Junior High is a reflection of how our school system often fails second language learners as they move into the upper grades. Students face much more academically challenging material, and often they are not provided with enough support to successfully negotiate conceptual and linguistic constructs across two languages. Too often it is assumed, without any real data to support these assumptions, that second language learners no longer need native language support or sheltering techniques to succeed in English. Or worse, as in evidence at Green, teachers view learning solely through English linguistic and hegemonic lenses which foster the ridiculous assumption that second language learners simply are not "capable" of handling rigorous material. Compounding the problem is a lack of understanding of how the socio-cultural and socio-linguistic milieu that surrounds students outside of the school context affects the ways they use language and construct knowledge. [This permits] teachers to dismiss the funds of knowledge and support which parents give to their children as non-existent or insufficient, at best.

—College Instructor

Home and School: The Myth That Parents Don't Care

A major theme in this case relates to home–school relationships. With little information available to teachers and little support for gathering more, misperception of parents from diverse linguistic and cultural backgrounds abounds. In this case, one teacher took the necessary step to try to get to know a student and her family. To do so meant meeting the challenge of communicating with parents who do not speak English. Respondents to this case who were able to communicate in a language other than English took it for granted that such communication could be easily established. But when teachers and administrators do not share a language with their students, they must reach out in cooperation with bilingual community members and agencies to accomplish this goal. Several aspects to the domain of home–school relationships are explored next.

Many immigrant families do not regularly visit the school, not knowing that parent involvement is an expectation commonly held by U.S. teachers and other school personnel. Parents' absence from the school building is interpreted to mean a lack of caring, when in reality, they may be staying away as a sign of respect or out of the desire to not interfere with the work of the teachers. A lack of confidence in being able to communicate with teachers and other school personnel may also inhibit parental interaction. This has resulted in the pervasive negative stereotype that immigrant parents can't or won't support their children's academic development.

I am not ashamed to admit that I once too thought that parents of second language learners did not care about the children's abilities and were, for a lack of a better word, lazy when it came to their children. I had the privilege to observe and conduct parent–teacher conferences last semester. These parents took time out of their busy, busy days to meet with teachers, asked what they could do to help and even asked about accountability! This really touched me because of my prior schema regarding second language parents.

—Teacher

Another common fallacy that was addressed in the case study is that second language parents do not care about education. Many of my students' parents do not always attend parent teacher conferences, but it in no way means that they do not care about their child's education. Many of them are working more than one job. Some are living in a single family home with a number of families. And quite often, they do not speak the same language as the teachers. Even more importantly they believe that there are two domains, [home and school] and do not feel that they can cross into the other. But that does not mean that they do not aid in the education of their children.

—Fifth Grade Teacher

I found it interesting that Jane was surprised by Marisa's personality outside of the school. It was almost as if she realized how discriminatory she and her school had been towards Marisa and was embarrassed. It also reminded me of the article by McIntosh, *White Privilege* (1989) because Jane (although it isn't specified) seems to come from the class of privilege. We see her attitudes expressed when she assumes Marisa prefers English, that she is fluent, and that because Marisa struggled in school her family wouldn't have books and magazines in their homes.

—Prospective Bilingual Teacher

The idea that the parents of second language learners are not interested is clearly a fallacy. I have a classroom that is three-fourths Spanish-speaking families and all but one of those families came to parent–teacher conferences. When I have a behavioral or academic issue I feel comfortable and supported when I call home. I am confident that when I inform parents of the expectations that I have, they will become my partners in the education of their children. They are hungry for materials in Spanish, and encourage their children to be successful. If anything prevents parents from full participation it is fear of confronting the school in a language that is not always valued, and not being able to advocate for their children in a language that they can speak. These families have a strong tradition of commitment to their families, but are not provided with resources to implement what is necessary.

—Bilingual Teacher

As for Jane's situation, I can't say that I relate. I feel that at my school, we are all very dedicated to the success of all students. We understand theories of language acquisition. Although there is certainly more that we could learn, we are educated in methods of teaching a second language. We understand that many families of lower socioeconomic status often hold multiple jobs and as a result find it difficult to be with their children as much as those of the middle and upper classes. (That's not to say that all families of middle and upper socioeconomic status spend more time with their children, but they may have more time available.) We also understand that people have different ways of "being with" their children. We understand that our families are dedicated to the success and happiness of their children.

—Bilingual Teacher–English component

Jane remarked that teachers "constantly blamed parents' lack of interest in their children's education for the fact that they didn't succeed." Unfortunately, I think that this attitude is very common. I think that out of frustration, educators are quick to say that parents just don't care. It is very easy to attribute parents' lack of involvement in parent–teacher conferences and school functions to an indifference to their child's education. I have taught for three years, and in that time I can honestly not think of one parent who didn't care. After home visits, many phone calls and parent teacher conferences at odd hours. I have found that most parents who are unable to attend school activities work 2–3 jobs, work odd hours, may not have a car, feel intimidated about asking how to help their child because they themselves have a very limited education. However, it is very rare that a parent truly doesn't care. I have found that a little persistence in contacting the family is usually all that is needed to understand how parents support their child, and to find out what parents need from the teacher in order to help their child succeed in school.

—Teacher

With children we are trained to ask: "What might be going on to prompt this change or initiate this new behavior?" Why would we fail to ask that question in relation to parents' circumstances as well?

—Master's Candidate

Roles That Parents Can Play

Many readers suggested that despite any language barriers that might exist, parents could be enlisted as allies in the education of their children.

> Parents have valuable insights into their children's abilities, strengths, weaknesses, sensitivities, etc. Their participation should be encouraged and valued as the necessity and treasure that it is.
>
> —Master's Candidate

> I would suggest to Marisa's family alternative ways that they can support Marisa's education. Providing Marisa with an environment conducive to studying, allowing Marisa to stay after school for additional tutoring, asking Marisa to discuss her daily learning with them in Spanish are a few examples. Letting the parents realize that there are many ways to support Marisa's education will help them to continue guiding her throughout her career without feeling inadequate with their own abilities.
>
> —Teacher

Make the Effort to Reach Out

Whereas most respondents acknowledged the challenges that linguistic and cultural diversity pose in establishing home school links, they still felt that it is incumbent on both individual teachers and schools to the make the effort to get to know students and their families in order to enlist their support.

> Jane actually pondered the meaning of what she observed in the home, instead of going with preconceived notions. More parent outreach could help other teachers feel more connected to the students' lives.
>
> —Secondary ESL Teacher

> Too often you hear that it is difficult for the Junior High and High School teachers to make contact with the parents because they have so many students as compared to the elementary teachers who only have 25 students. This is a cop out! I have just as many students as they do if you figure out all the subjects the elementary teachers are teaching—math, science, social studies, language/writing, and reading. All these subjects require a great deal of time and planning. They are usually only planning for one subject such as science. I personally believe that they can and should be making contact with parents and as Jane mentioned these are the "critical years" when many students drop out. At this time, they need extra support and contact with the home, so the students can make a good choice.
>
> —Teacher

Jane has also learned a social lesson, which is that it is possible to include parents in the education of their children, and, further, that what looks like parental neglect may be a longing to be involved, thwarted by language and cultural misunderstanding. When Jane hears her colleagues lament the disengagement of Hispanic parents, hopefully she will retell her encounter with Marisa's family as an example of how being proactive can make a difference.

—Prospective Teacher

One of the most effective ways to better get to know students and their families is to visit them at home. This outreach strategy presents many challenges to teachers.

This teacher was willing to go and speak to her students' parents. Usually this only happens during parent–teacher conferences. I believe that a visit to our student's home tells us volumes about a child. I did my student teaching at a school that did home visits to all of their students in the beginning of the year. From these visits I learned why one student was always so tired. He had to share a room with two brothers and an uncle who drank. This is only one example, but we need to take the time to get to know not only our students, but their parents, as well. If we know the parents hopefully we can help them to help their children at home. If children are getting help at home too, they are seeing that their parents put an importance on their schoolwork and hopefully they will see the importance of school and doing a good job.

—Graduate Student

Teachers can gain a tremendous amount of practical information by doing a home visit or even by driving through the local neighborhoods of their schools. Home visits can enlighten a teacher as to the amount of literacy materials in the home, what the parents' work situations are, how the child communicates and responds when in familiar surroundings, and how the school can better help the families and their children be successful.

—Bilingual Teacher

Building on the Strengths of Students and Their Families

A final theme that emerged from the responses to this case related to the need to build on the assets of students and their families. Comments focused both on the particular strengths that Marisa displayed and more generally on the role of parents and their ability to support students' work in school through their primary language at home.

Someone needs to help Marisa find outlets for the development of her other talents as well. She has leadership and athletic skills that could be developed through participation on a soccer team, either school or community based. She also would be an asset in a student leadership role such as tutoring younger children, student council, or student volunteer activities in the community. Marisa needs to be consulted as to where her interests lie to encourage her to follow-up on this. Participation in these activities can help develop her self-esteem, which supports academic achievement.

—Middle School ESL Teacher

One of the keys to success in school that helps prevent dropping-out is getting students involved. Once students experience success, consider their presence to be important, and have their strengths validated they will be less likely to leave. Marisa's leadership could be her greatest natural strength.

—Prospective Teacher

When "support" is narrowly defined as completing homework assignments in English, then, indeed, parents may be unable to help. However, if support is defined more broadly as contributing to students' overall linguistic and conceptual development, then parents can play an important role in furthering their children's academic success regardless of their level of English proficiency. Parents can be made aware of the themes and concepts their children are studying in school, and reinforce these ideas and discuss them with their child in the child's primary language.

One of the first misconceptions that this particular teacher had was that Marisa's progress was adversely affected by an apparent lack of participation on the part of the family. Homework was not routinely returned, or it was done haphazardly. Marisa clearly demonstrated ability but her product was not reflecting this. There is also the belief that lack of participation clearly points to lack of interest in a child's education on the part of the parents. I have worked extensively with second language learners and neither one of these ideas is valid. Homework that is sent home in the native language is done with the same regularity as the homework of the monolingual English children.

—Third Grade Teacher

It is also important that Marisa continues to develop academic vocabulary in her native language. Her parents appear to be very supportive. Jane could ask Marisa to discuss the meaning of abstract words, such as democracy and freedom, with her parents at home. This way Marisa could gain a better understanding of the word and would be learning more about her parents' experience. Marisa will then be able to apply this new information to her studies.

—Prospective Teacher

For some respondents, the issues raised by Marisa's situation highlight the need for teachers to actively affirm the diversity among their students. They suggest that common understandings regarding students' strengths and potential need to be built among all school personnel. Many felt that to truly reflect an asset orientation teachers must create a classroom community where commonalties are recognized and diversity is celebrated.

Jane should maintain her high expectations of Marisa. There is nothing that indicates otherwise. Marisa will sense if she's been "demoted," and her attitudes about school and learning will be adversely affected. Jane has to remain sensitive to the fact that she is dealing with a young student whose world is divided. By creating a classroom environment where diversity is recognized and celebrated Jane will be taking a step towards closing that gap. Marisa, as well as other students, should be encouraged to enrich the classroom discussions and environment by offering their experiences and insights. Overall, they should be valued and recognized for who they are.

—Prospective Teacher

I am reminded of what I already claim to know. It is essential to recognize the individual as a whole—*including* culture, language, learning style, etc.

—Master's Candidate

To me, the underlying message of this case study, and many situations that I have lived through, is just a need for understanding. We are all here, on this planet, in this country, more or less doing and wanting the same things, and yet no one really understands each other. Understanding, respecting and tolerating each other, to me, seems like an easy task to accomplish, but the truth is, we have a long way to go.

—Elementary Bilingual Teacher

READER REACTIONS TO "MARISA'S PROSPECTS"

SUMMARY AND ADDITIONAL QUESTIONS

First-generation students like Marisa are especially vulnerable in school. They and their families may be unfamiliar with U.S. schools and their requirements. It is easy for them to get caught between the differing expectations and norms that may exist between home and school. When teachers and students come from divergent backgrounds, as is the case in most linguistically diverse schools, it is easy to misinterpret behaviors according to one's own experiences. Teachers' caseloads at the secondary level can make the reality of getting to know students and their families individually seem unreasonable. When closer contact is lacking, it is easy to make faulty assumptions. There is a tendency, for example, to view parental absence from schools as signaling a lack of caring on their part. However, an equally valid alternative perspective would suggest that this might be a result of other reasons, such as having no flexibility at work.

All students develop some sort of coping mechanism to deal with the stresses of living in two worlds. Very often parents do lack the necessary skills in English to help their children with schoolwork in English. If schools do not actively reach out to assist students they will be left to navigate the cultural rift on their own. Some strategies are more effective than others as exemplified by Marisa's decision to translate all of her work on her own. Although this clearly demonstrated her willingness to do whatever it would take to complete her work, without anyone to guide her these efforts were not helping her to achieve her goals.

It is important to consider ways that schools can build on the students' strengths and those of their families. To this end consider the following questions:

- How can teachers come to recognize the full set of strengths that second language learners bring to the classroom setting and their efforts to learn and succeed?
- How can teachers demonstrate that they value students and the language and culture they bring with them to the classroom?
- What can schools do to value parents' contributions at home and to encourage parents to help with their children's conceptual development using their primary language?
- What approach is most likely to promote lasting change, top down or bottom up?

- To what extent is it up to individual teachers to take responsibility for gathering information about issues of concern to all?
- How far should an individual teacher go in terms of time commitment? Should teachers' efforts towards establishing relationships with parents be part of the teacher evaluation process?
- How can teachers with large numbers of students get to know them on an individual basis, especially if they don't speak the students' languages? Is it reasonable to require that teachers conduct home visits? If so, what structures are necessary to facilitate their implementation?

INTRODUCTION TO CASE 3

This case study features a school whose growing linguistic diversity is compelling all teachers to rethink the organizational structure in their school. In the past at Randall Elementary, learners whose home language is Spanish have only been assigned to one of three bilingual teachers provided by the district. These three teachers worked to meet all the students' needs in both their first and second language. Because of the increasing numbers of students and a lack of bilingual personnel, this method of assigning students is no longer feasible. Monolingual English-speaking teachers who have not before had to work directly with second language learners will now need to share responsibility for their instruction. These changes have the potential to either split the staff apart or to revitalize the school as a whole. The case focuses on the uncertainties this situation raises for a third grade, English-only teacher, and her experiences in this transition. Issues raised include: What is the total staff responsibility to serve all of its learners? What is the role of a monolingual English-speaking teacher with regard to the education of linguistically diverse students? How can teachers be successful in such changes? What professional preparation is needed to help all teachers feel competent in this arena?

CASE 3: "FRIENDSHIP, PROFESSIONALISM, AND PROGRAMS"

Juana and Laura are friends. They work together at Randall Elementary where, over the past few years, the community surrounding the school has been changing dramatically. Tensions associated with these changes have made working at Randall Elementary a stressful experience for both teachers. Where the community was once primarily white working class, it is now approximately 60% Latino and 40% white. The Latino families are primarily Mexican and approximately 45% of the students are new English learners. All of the Latino children, however, live in a bilingual environment.

Laura is a third grade teacher. She remembers Randall Elementary School before the changes in the student population. When she first came to the school it was all white. At that time there was a fairly clear dividing line between the white community to the north, the Latino community to the west, and the African-American community to the east. Each of these neighborhoods had their own community school. And, although there had always been voices pushing for greater integration, people from each of the communities seemed happy to stay with their own. Over the past 5 years, however, the white community has begun to shrink whereas the minority population has increased. The higher paying factory jobs have moved out of the area and with them many of the white workers who were employed there. In their place, several hotels and restaurants have opened nearby attracting more and more Latino families for whom service jobs are a major entry into the workforce. As the community has changed so have the students at Randall Elementary.

Laura considers herself a life-long learner. She feels that it is important to continually find ways to improve her knowledge about the students she teaches, and her skills to reach them effectively. Therefore, when the school began to change, she felt the need to take classes in multicultural education, and has even taken a class in teaching English as a Second Language. From these classes she learned that there are various types of programs that can be organized for students from linguistically diverse backgrounds. These include early exit, sheltered, immersion, and two-way bilingual. What has concerned her most about the changes at Randall Elementary is that although the demography of the students has changed, very little else about the school has changed. Four years ago when the school started hiring bilingual teachers, she along with many of her monolingual colleagues had grave misgivings. It seemed to them that what the students needed was more English, not less. Many of the teachers, however, either could not or would not admit to their limited knowledge in this area, and seemed to be intimidated by their lack of understanding of the families, their culture, and language. Consequently, they backed off and neither pursued nor raised the linguistic and educational issues the change had brought. In fact, because many of the monolingual teachers did feel inadequate, they were more than happy to turn over responsibility for these learners to the bilingual staff. But, as the numbers of second language English learners in the school has grown, it has become evident to everyone that this strategy is no longer viable. The principal has been aware of the problems but because his administration program did not prepare him to work with linguistically and culturally diverse communities either, he has been at a loss for what to do. To address these issues, he has decided to hold a faculty retreat on the topic.

Although no expert, Laura has learned a few things about second language acquisition and as a result she feels that a lot of curricular changes need to be made. She knows that Randall Elementary needs much more shared responsibility for students and greater coordination of curriculum.

She has many friends on the staff, however, and is reluctant to voice her concerns. Teachers have always worked independently at Randall, and although they have always been cordial to each other and participated as a team in school-wide functions, they have always been responsible for their *own* classroom instruction.

Juana is one of the only two ethnically diverse teachers at Randall Elementary, and one of the three bilingual teachers hired. What has made Randall Elementary a difficult experience for Juana is that although she was hired because she is bilingual, there has been very little organization, discussion, program planning, or support in response to the demographic changes occurring at the school. Virtually all issues related to the language minority students are referred to the three bilingual teachers because they are the only ones on staff who have had instruction in first and second language acquisition. It seems to Juana that the other teachers just want to ignore these students. This is her first teaching position and she feels torn between what she perceives as the needs of the bilingual students, wanting to be seen as part of the staff, and her obligation to speak up about the lack of a school-wide strategy.

Juana has both English monolingual and new English learners in her third grade class. She is, therefore, responsible for all areas of the curriculum, in both languages. Because of the limited bilingual staff in the district, the program at Randall is early exit. In K–2 the Spanish-speaking students in the bilingual program are receiving most of their instruction in their first language. By third grade, however, most children are reading and writing well in their first language, are beginning formal English reading, and are also receiving much of their content in English. On a typical day Juana does reading and math groups in Spanish and in English. She conducts science and social studies lessons in English, but also regularly conducts content lessons in the native language to assure that the Spanish speakers have the opportunity to develop new concepts fully. Additionally, she teaches English as a second language lessons every day. It is hard for Juana to deal with all of the instructional issues that arise in both languages. In order to teach social studies, science and math in the students' primary language, she must prepare curriculum materials that are not available to her in the school. She also often has to modify the materials in English so that they are understandable to the second language learners. It's a tremendous job and she often just doesn't know if she can keep up.

Juana also worries a great deal about what happens when students are moved out of the bilingual program. Being an early exit program, when students are considered "ready" they are transferred into the all-English classes. For most of these students this occurs at fourth grade. Although first language speakers of Spanish have developed a good deal of competence in English (strong oral English and an initial comfort level with English literacy) it is clear that they have not yet had enough time to become fully proficient in English.

When they go into the all-English classes, however, teachers do not know how to continue supporting these second language learners in order to ensure their success. When students who have attained some fluency in English, but who continue to need support to become fully native-like English speakers are put into all English classes they often fall behind the monolingual English speakers. Juana sees some of her brightest students struggling in areas where they could easily succeed if they were given appropriate support. Teachers often assume that students have been exited from the bilingual program because they are fully proficient and not because of imposed time limits. They are not aware of these students' need for continued English language development support. Consequently, they often miss opportunities to engage and support these students. Of the monolingual English teachers, only Juana's friend Laura has had any experience in this area, and given the way the school is structured she does not work with second language learners at all.

Because of this situation, Latino parents often have come to Juana very worried about their children's progress and anxious about their future. These parents are afraid to talk to the monolingual English teachers and they express to her their feeling of discomfort about visiting the school. Juana also worries when, in the lounge, other teachers bemoan the fact that no matter what they try, these students never seem to catch up. Although they don't say it in front of her, she knows many of them feel that she and the other bilingual teachers are doing the students a disservice by teaching them in their primary language. What is particularly frustrating to her is that many of them are excellent teachers of monolingual English students. But they do not see the importance of helping students of another native language group to develop a strong primary language foundation. Because they are good teachers, she knows they could readily learn how to better support the second language learners in their classrooms, but they don't seem to want to and they don't seem to care.

Generally, Laura has not had to deal with the issues that worry Juana because only the bilingual teachers have been assigned to work with bilingual students. All she really knows is that fourth grade all-English teachers often complain about how the students who come from the bilingual classes are not functioning as well as the native English speakers. Because she really doesn't know what and how Juana teaches, she feels uncomfortable about criticizing the bilingual program. And, although it seems logical to her that students be able to use their first language for learning, she and Juana have never talked about it.

District-wide, testing is done at the fourth grade and scores at Randall Elementary have not been good. The faculty now needs to discuss in earnest how to improve their program. The bilingual teachers are upset. They feel they cannot do justice to all of their instructional responsibilities. They have both Spanish speakers and monolingual English speakers assigned to their classrooms and, therefore, have to deal with the entire curriculum in both languages. They also feel that it is unfair that teachers who teach only monolingual English speakers have no responsibility for second language learners, even though these students make up a significant portion of the school population. In addition, they have also heard the fourth grade teachers' criticisms and feel that if those teachers understood the second language development process and knew how to support these learners in their classroom, the problems would be alleviated.

The three bilingual teachers want monolingual English teachers to team teach with them so that the responsibility for English as a second language development is shared. They feel this would help Randall Elementary have a stronger program, and that increased understanding and participation would especially benefit students when they moved from the bilingual program to the all-English program. Additionally, teachers and families would have more opportunity to share across cultures and become more comfortable with each other. Perhaps monolingual English speaking students might also one day have the opportunity to become bilingual.

Juana has asked Laura if she would be willing to team with her. For many reasons Laura finds this a difficult position to be in. She knows the bilingual teachers are right, there are too many children to be served only by them, and that other teachers in the school have avoided getting involved. On the other hand, she has never had to teach second language learners and since she is not bilingual she is unsure how she could communicate effectively with these students. Her lack of knowledge about the culture, language, and needs of the Latino children makes her feel very inadequate.

Also, Laura is afraid of alienating herself from other teachers. Already, because of her friendship with Juana and the fact that she has shown an interest in learning more about second language acquisition and multicultural education, Laura has sensed a coolness from some of her colleagues. She worries that a decision to become more involved in these issues might set her apart from the rest of the staff.

There is also the issue of the bilingual education itself. Laura understands that second language learners need a different presentation of material, but she is afraid that if she expresses any reservations about the use of the primary language itself, she will be thought of as intolerant or insensitive. She doesn't see herself this way, but she thinks the bilingual teachers' use of Spanish needs to be more balanced with English. She realizes that it is, in part, her own insecurity about not knowing the students' language and her inability to understand them when they speak to each other that makes her nervous about her ability to help them learn.

Finally, Laura is also hesitant because she has always enjoyed her absolute freedom in the classroom. In all the schools where she has worked principals have pretty much left teachers alone. Although she missed the collegial interactions she thought would be part of teaching, she has learned to appreciate her autonomy. If she were to team teach, she would have to work collaboratively, thereby giving up some of her freedom. And, what if she and Juana did not get along, or found that their ways of organizing instruction, their goals for students, and their classroom management and methods of discipline weren't compatible. She is afraid that not only her teaching might be compromised but that their friendship would be ruined, as well.

The principal's decision to have a retreat on the subject has made it necessary for Laura to take a stand. She has agonized over this decision, but the bottom line for her is that the quality of instruction for students could be significantly improved, and this outweighs her personal reservations and apprehensions. A couple of days before the retreat, Laura tells Juana that she is willing to team teach with her. She also shares her reservations with Juana, including those about the bilingual program. As she talks to Juana she realizes that it matters to her that these concerns get out on the table, and they be discussed by the whole faculty. She tells Juana that she is hoping to present them during the upcoming meeting. They both agree that they hope *all* the teachers will be willing to openly share their concerns and positively join in the effort to improve Randall Elementary's program. With a good deal of uneasiness Laura prepares for the retreat.

How would you respond to Laura's thoughts and concerns?

You are one of Laura's colleagues at another school in the district. She has called you to talk things over. What would you advise her?

READER REACTIONS TO
LAURA AND JUANA'S SITUATION

REACTIONS TO "FRIENDSHIP, PROFESSIONALISM, AND PROGRAMS"

The theme of change and resistance evident in each of the cases thus far is again echoed here. Respondents to this case study highlight the "us and them" attitudes that often permeate schools that serve second language learners. The comments address the error in placing the entire responsibility for these students' academic success solely on the staff members who can communicate with the children and their families. They challenge the idea that a small number of teachers could possibly handle all the students who need second language services. They underscore the importance of whole school involvement to meet the needs of the diverse communities that the school serves.

Readers of this case point out that because teachers generally cannot choose who their students are, they must be prepared to teach all students who arrive in their classrooms. Respondents also see that it is the responsibility of individual teachers who are aware of what must be done to step forward and take on leadership roles.

Many individuals also addressed the debate over whether monolingual English speaking teachers can effectively work with non-English speaking students. There were varied perceptions of the role of the primary language and whether students can attain academic success if they do or don't have access to their primary language in instruction.

Readers described the dangers of school personnel working in isolation and a need for solutions that take a school-wide approach with strong leadership from the principal. Their comments reflect the tension that arises when teachers' autonomy is seemingly threatened by the kinds of structures required to respond to the needs of a more linguistically diverse population. Team teaching is examined and respondents address its pros and cons and offer advice for making it work.

Confronting the Demographic Shift

One of the most prevalent themes in the responses to this case was *face reality and face your fears*. Teachers have to recognize and confront the changing demographics head on, and teach in ways that will accommodate the students who are actually in their classrooms. Most teachers are monolingual English speakers from the dominant culture. Nonetheless, they have the responsibility to become familiar with their students and find ways to interact successfully with them. Part of the resistance to change was seen as reflecting individual teacher's fears of difference on several levels. Differences with their students, fear of standing out from their peers, fears of moving beyond their current zones of comfort.

Laura's thoughts and concerns are very real in talking about schools that are experiencing a rapidly changing community. In this sort of context, the staff at a school may begin to experience, perhaps for the first time, students who are culturally and linguistically different from themselves. When this situation arises, so do real anxieties, fears, and difficulties.

—Graduate Student

I see one of the biggest problems at Randall Elementary being its lack of organization around meeting the needs of second language learners. The split between the regular ed and bilingual ed teachers is hurtful to everyone, as it serves to make teachers feel isolated and unsupported and definitely does not give the students the support that they need to succeed academically. It seems that there is an overall feeling of individualism that leads to isolation among the staff in the school, and that this isolation leads to a sense of confusion and even resentment among the teachers.

—Graduate Student

I believe Laura has made the only proper decision. Her anxieties about losing popularity among fellow educators because of her stand seem ridiculous in the face of what the children have to lose. Her school is filled with children who need different kinds of instruction than was needed by the students of the school's past. If the needs of the children change, then the teachers must change to help fill those needs.

—Prospective Teacher

The concerns raised by Laura have implications for more than just teaching practices. They deal with the larger sociopolitical context within which Randall Elementary operates. Just training teachers in ESL techniques and the importance of primary language foundations is not enough. It seems that many of the teachers need to broaden their personal horizons and views of minority cultures, and the special needs and richness they bring to school. I would go so far as to say that if teachers are not willing to be trained in how to better serve the needs of the school population, they should be urged to find employment elsewhere.

—Second Year Elementary Teacher

Laura cannot afford to "ignore" this population simply because she comes from a different cultural and linguistic background. As a colleague, I would validate her concern and encourage her to take positive steps to "bridge the gap" between the home culture of her students and the school culture.

—Prospective Teacher

The principal's decision to have the retreat is the beginning of communication. During the retreat it would be important for Laura, Juana and the rest of the staff to come together and build a positive sense of community. They need to begin discussion with "we as a staff" not "us and them," "bilingual vs. nonbilingual."

—Teacher

The planned retreat is an excellent opportunity for unifying themes and purposes of the school and staff. Initially, she may sense some "coolness" from certain members of the staff (which will likely go away once they are educated on the issues of bilingual education) but she must stay focused on her purposes for teaching. As educators, we must all keep ourselves educated and "up to date." Laura and the rest of the staff have a responsibility to learn how to effectively teach all of the students in the school. Instruction must be tailored to fit the children, and Laura and the bilingual teachers are in a prime position to lead the staff in remembering this.

—Prospective Teacher

I would also recommend reading Vivian Paley (1989), a white teacher who writes about teaching students from other cultures than herself. This literature may provide Laura with the beauty of the situation and to feel the humanness of teaching. Laura could see the possibilities and commonality in Paley's writings in dealing with this profession.

—Teacher Working on ESL Certification

Some readers suggested that under our educational system public schools should provide students a free and appropriate education that matches their needs. They pointed to legal guidelines that are intended to protect the rights of all children to receive an equitable education and recommended that they should be adhered to.

As changes occur in a school district and children from diverse backgrounds who speak a different language begin to attend the school, it is imperative that the school recognize the changes and amend the curriculum accordingly. Furthermore, Office for Civil Rights guidelines designed to remedy discrimination as an outcome of the case Lau v. Nichols in 1974 state:

> Districts must describe the diagnostic/prescriptive measures to be used to identify the nature and extent of each student's educational needs and then prescribe an educational program utilizing the most effective teaching style to satisfy the diagnosed educational needs. . . . (They) must bring linguistically/ culturally different students to the educational performance levels [of the district and] must not be operated, divorced or isolated from those educational objectives established for the students in the regular program. (Notes from class lecture on legal guidelines for working with second language learners.)
>
> —Master's Candidate

Laura should feel confident to present this case to the Office of Civil Rights (OCR). As of now Randall Elementary is clearly not meeting the needs of the language minority population, which at Randall represents the majority. Perhaps Laura needs to speak to an Office of Civil Rights representative before the retreat to gain more ammo for her presentation.

—Upper Elementary Teacher

It's Time to Act

Many individuals saw it as Laura's responsibility to act on the knowledge about second language acquisition and appropriate instruction that she had gained in her coursework. Given the climate in the building and the number of teachers lacking knowledge, they felt that Laura had no choice but to take on a leadership role. She should put the needs of her students first, despite any misgivings she might have about being vocal.

> I thoroughly believe that teachers must speak out about their concerns and thoughts, and take a stand for their students. Laura was correct in deciding to put things out on the table along with the other teachers, and discuss the general concerns teachers may have in this situation. My impression is that Laura needs to hear from other teachers who may be having similar dilemmas and getting things out in the open. In reality, it is a question about the needs of students and how best together, the staff and the school principal can help clarify their misconceptions and help improve the school's program.
>
> —Elementary Bilingual Teacher–Spanish Component

Just as Laura feels inadequate to fully deal with the changes at her school, the other teachers probably do too—except they know even less about effectively educating linguistically diverse students than Laura does. Laura doesn't need to allow that gap of knowledge to widen. She can be proactive and share what she has learned with her colleagues so they can join her in making changes, rather than feeling afraid because they are not part of the process and don't understand it.

—Elementary Bilingual Teacher–English Component

I would say to Laura: you recognize the need for curricular changes, shared responsibility, and coordination of curriculum. Now you just need to be more willing to voice your concerns. You need to be an advocate for ALL the children regardless of whether you speak their language or not. Basically, you need to go with what you know is right in your heart—and that is help provide a quality education for all children regardless of their skin color, religion, or native tongue. But also remember that change is difficult, but it must be ten times as difficult for the second language learners at Randall who are struggling under the current program which is failing them. You need to gain a wider perspective—to step outside of the situation and look in from the outside. From out here the answers are very clear.

—Master's Candidate

If Laura's lack of experience about the culture, language, and needs of the Latino children makes her feel inadequate, this concern should be all the more reason to initiate collaboration with her friend Juana and other members of the Latino community so that she can begin to build her knowledge. Most likely, many of the other white teachers in Laura's school have similar feelings of inadequacy and, even if not, could really benefit from further education about the Latino community and Latino students' cognitive, linguistic, social, and academic needs.

Also, Laura needs to become an advocate for the second language learners at Randall Elementary. I think her desire to be a life-long learner/teacher is admirable, but this role involves a lot of responsibility. Personally, I feel Laura, as a learner/teacher, has the moral responsibility to teach every student who enters her classroom as well as act an ally for change for students who are not receiving an education which best meets their needs. I believe Laura's fears of jeopardizing her friendship with Juana, or with her other colleagues for that matter, are trivial when one considers the vast injustice that is being served to second language learners through Randall's present program.

—Second Year Teacher

I would advise Laura to listen to her own words. She stated that "the bottom line is that the quality of student instruction could be improved." It is her responsibility as a teacher to give all students an equal opportunity. I would advise her to invite her colleagues to work with her in becoming a community of learners. In educating themselves, shared concerns and uncertainties will likely dissipate. Despite her concerns, Laura has a primary responsibility to the children and families of the school. The entire staff has the same responsibility. Laura could use this opportunity to renew their awareness of this.

—Prospective Teacher

Some respondents made reference to the fact that as a white teacher, Laura is in a better position to be heard than Juana. One comment in particular illustrates how who you are, affects how you are heard, and how you are perceived. It also illustrates the inequalities that permeate professional relationships as a result of negative attitudes toward, and the devaluing of the opinions of people of color.

Laura is in the perfect position to effect change at Randall Elementary. She's probably fairly young, presumably white, and is beginning to see that schools are not exactly "the great equalizer" that Horace Mann envisioned. While her friend Juana better understands the issues that have arisen at Randall due to the demographic changes, it is unfortunate that her opinions at the teacher retreat will probably be received differently than those same opinions expressed by Laura. Since Juana has a similar cultural background to the children she is trying to help, she will be seen as having a "personal agenda" that can be discounted more easily. Laura is in a better position to be heard by the staff; a white, male principal would be even more convincing. The best approach, however, would be for the principal to invite a guest speaker to the retreat—a person who has experienced and adapted successfully to a similar demographic shift. No matter how risky, Laura and Juana need to present their plan to team teach.

—Teacher in Master's Program

Which Language Is Best?

A major focus of the commentary was on the use and role of Spanish in instruction. The debate over bilingual education has been going on for decades and continues to dominate discussion over how best to help English language learners become successful in school. In several states, voters have had to consider ballot initiatives that would eliminate the use of a language other than English for instruction and in many cases force a one-year program of segregated structured immersion in English.

The following quotes are posted on the Web site of English for the Children (2004), an organization dedicated to the elimination of bilingual education in the United States (http://onenation.org). They are taken from letters to the editor printed in newspapers over the past few years, as well as the personal stories of several immigrants. They all strongly object to the use of students' native language in instruction in school.

There is everything to celebrate about the rising test scores of Hispanic students in English-speaking classrooms in California (front page, Aug. 20, 2000). The bilingual approach was both linguistically and socially misguided right from the outset, and many former bilingual teachers like me did not take long to realize its pedagogic flaws.

There is no reason these children cannot retain their native language as long as they are exposed to it at home. Their Spanish vocabulary may suffer while their English one grows, but the syntactic matrixes of both languages can and will coexist, thrive individually and even reinforce and supplement each other.

—*New York Times* (Letters), Wednesday, August 23, 2000

Teachers and teachers-in-training are being BRAINWASHED by education professors into thinking that these ineffective methods and unproven theories constitute sound educational practice. The sad fact is, most teacher candidates are not intelligent enough or independent-minded enough to realize that they are being brainwashed. I saw my classmates in the credential program react enthusiastically to ideas that were senseless and harmful. Many elementary teachers are not particularly intellectually inclined and have chosen teaching as a profession because they love working with children, not because they believe in the importance of a substantive education. Comments from a substitute teacher re. bilingual ed and education in general.

—Your Stories: Comments from a Substitute Teacher
Name Withheld—Monday, October 5, 1998

In 1923, when I started first grade at the Sarah B. Cooper school in San Francisco, I and several other youngsters, although all natives of California, spoke no English. . . . We had a great need—the need to communicate with each other and in no time, two weeks I believe, we began to talk and point and play together in a language different than the one we had known from birth and as we gained confidence in this new language, we ran and played and even learned the Pledge of Allegiance. Finally we belonged and it felt good. What was so good was that we now could converse in English as well as in our mother tongue. The moral of this very true story is that if we could learn so well back in 1923, the immigrant children of the 1990's can do it too.

       —Your Stories: My story for what it's worth, May 19, 1998

I also came from a background of only knowing Spanish, until I started school in Los Angeles back in 1969 where the teacher only spoke English. I remember trying to understand what was going on and eventually learning English so well that I went on to graduate from high school without ever retreating into any kind of shell.

    In fact, without the benefit of bilingual education I can speak English with barely an accent. My four brothers are also responsible adult professionals who are proficient in both languages. Bilingual education puts a child at a disadvantage, and the best way to learn English is to totally submerge that child in the language. It worked for me and I'm sure it worked for many other people who learned English in this way.

       —*Long Beach Press-Telegram* (Letters), Sunday, March 1, 1998

Starting with the definition of a nation as a stable community of people with a territory, history, culture, and language in common, I strongly believe that we should support and encourage the immigrant children to master the English language in order to become an integral part of this nation.

       —Your Stories: An Israeli in Silicon Valley,
       Wednesday, February 25, 1998

In contrast, not one of the over 100 teachers, graduate students, support personnel, and administrators who read and responded to this case objected directly to the proposed use of Spanish in instruction. Many individuals could understand the monolingual English teachers' point of view. However, they saw teaching in the students' home language as a means to facilitate English language acquisition by strengthening students' literacy and conceptual skills, skills that they then transfer to their learning of English.

Laura, like many of the monolingual teachers, feels that the children need more English, which is true to the extent that in the U.S., English is the language of power. But they need to understand that the best way in my opinion to that goal is to develop literacy in a primary language. Children will acquire much more English in transferring knowledge from language one to another than in starting from scratch at 6, 7, or 8 and trying to "keep up" with monolingual classmates. The effects of this coupled with alienation from culture and family, ultimately leading to a loss of identity, will destroy the greatest asset a child has, and that is motivation to learn.

       —Prospective Teacher

Laura must be aware that the role of the primary language for students acquiring English is vital in the development and transfer to the second. Her belief that it must be more balanced, suggests that Laura does not fully understand the rationale for more time spent in primary language during the early elementary opposed to the second. Because she is worried that students are not developing the appropriate English skills to be successful in the later grades and monolingual English classrooms, she attributes this problem to "too much" primary language instruction in the early years. However, this is a criticism of most bilingual programs by advocates of the English-Only movement. I would thoroughly agree with Laura, on the other hand that students need access to academic English in order to be successful, and that we are doing students a disservice to them if we fail to provide these opportunities in our instruction.

—Bilingual Teacher–Spanish component

The quality of resources in multilingual classrooms is uneven. Teachers' general level of awareness in Randall Elementary is very low. Their knowledge of the benefits of linguistic diversity—for individual children and for society as a whole—is limited and their focus is often exclusively on English. Bilingual Education for language minority students offers second language development and, at the same time, provides students with opportunity to acquire subject matter knowledge in the primary language and to stimulate cognitive development. Effectiveness should not be judged only on linguistic criteria as the achievement in English literacy skills is strongly related to the extent of development of the first language literacy skills.

—Teacher

Regarding hesitations about L1 instruction. We are all familiar with the sociopolitical issues raised concerning native language instruction. However, I challenge Laura to define what she views as "equal opportunity for education." Is it about *participation* or compensation? It appears that Laura supports the participatory notion. Therefore, I would advise her to critically reflect on the larger societal structure and the power that language holds. I would encourage her to question the status quo as well as institutionalized assumptions about L1 instruction in order to reflect how L1 instructions gives students access to schooling and creates a participatory climate in which individual efforts may flourish.

—Prospective Teacher

Since Laura is afraid of being seen as insensitive, she needs to understand the process and time necessary for students to acquire English as their second language by doing research on her own or consulting professionals in this area. She also needs to learn about the importance of a strong foundation in the native language along with English (ESL) before students can be expected to be taught in English. Laura could have this question posed to her to make her really think about her position: If a student cannot speak or understand English (or with minimum competence), how is he/she expected to learn concepts that are abstract or conceptual for native English speakers? All of these issues are what Laura needs to understand before she draws any conclusions in how the bilingual classrooms are being taught.

—Teacher

I would advise Laura to seek out authoritative research to learn the positive effects of bilingual maintenance programs. I would assure her, as well, that as a fluent speaker of English, with proper ESL training and cultural sensitivity she will be an effective English and content teacher to second language learners, as long as they develop literacy skills in the language that they have already had thousands of hours of practice speaking. It is essential that monolingual English speaking teachers realize that it is much easier to transfer knowledge of one language for which one has much experience to learning a second language.

—Prospective Teacher

Although we expected more teachers to reject primary language use completely, hesitations among the readers regarding the use of students' first language in the school had to do specifically with the monolingual English teachers' inability to speak the language of their students.

To teach students who are second language learners does not require you to teach the target language, but rather that you have an awareness for how students learn a second language, what strategies would most benefit your student's needs, and developing a secure language rich environment where students have opportunities to use a variety of language functions in their second language.

—Bilingual Teacher–Spanish component

I can understand the different concerns and fears that you have regarding teaching second language learners, such as being insecure about communicating effectively; your lack of experience with their culture, language, and needs; and your fears of alienation from the monolingual teachers. In terms of lacking communication skills, I think that it is important to understand that effective team teaching does not require that you speak the student's primary language. In fact, some experts believe that it is important that teachers speak and teach English and Spanish in distinct blocks of time. In other words, it can be helpful for students if they are required to speak in English to get their needs met, instead of using Spanish as a crutch. . . . You should also consider the importance of talking to your principal and staff about setting aside staff development time to learn more about the culture, language and needs of your Latino students.

—First Year Teacher

Total School Approach

Most readers saw Laura and Juana's proposal as only a small step. Although a few respondents felt that Laura and Juana should take the plunge to lead the way, the more typical response was that the retreat should be just the beginning of a much more concerted, long-term effort toward school-wide change. There was a general recognition that the issue was much bigger than two teachers, and that some hard work would be required if the needs of all children at Randall were to be met. There was also almost unanimous agreement that the principal should lead such an effort.

Laura and Juana should gather together the accessible research on team teaching and make the announcement that they are going to be team teaching, and show the others how this will be more equitable for students and for teachers, and about their own feelings about what was happening in the school. Maybe the principal and the teachers would decide to make some major changes in the school. That would be great, but I think that all Juana and Laura can do is to present their case, the case of the school, and the research supporting their decision as clearly as possible and try to gain the support of other concerned teachers. At worst, school will be better for about sixty people. At best, the entire school will change in a way that will better for it's demographics and serve all its learners.

—Teacher

I do not believe that this school is going about the process correctly. Change needs to happen in an organized and planned manner. It does not happen in one meeting, or in one retreat. It seems to me that there are limited lines of communication in the school. It's almost as if two entirely different schools exist—one for the traditional students, and one for the "new" students. Things are assumed between these two groups and I am also quite sure that there is a lot of resentment between them especially around issues of workload, job security, and so on. To think that these two schools are going to come together and come up with a plan seems a bit naïve. But if the school is to come to grips and educate their children, they will have to come together and form a philosophy, mission statement, and strategy. To do this there is going to have to be a lot of dialogue, inservices, and training, on the population of students the school is now facing. The staff needs to be open-minded and willing to work together.

—Prospective Teacher

I would suggest that even though even one teacher who has taken the responsibility to educate themselves on the issues of bilingual education can accomplish alot, it is in fact, a school-wide responsibility. The entire school staff should be asking the question: How can we best organize ourselves and our resources to meet the students' needs? Although it is true that every effort should be made to be inclusive, supportive and understanding of people's fears, anyone who is not willing to ask that fundamental question does not belong at the school, nor, in my opinion, in the teaching profession. I would suggest to Laura that in addition to meeting with Juana, making some school visits and educating herself by reading up on the issues, she establish a dialogue with the principal, so that there is support for the decision to team teach, as well as a beginning sense of working together. The principal could then begin to feel a team of professionals interested in collaborating on the issues rather than factious undercurrents that breed distrust and alienation.

—Prospective Teacher

The issue at hand is not Laura. She is just one teacher in the community, who will and needs to play into the complete responsibility of the school's goal to serve their students. The problem is with the school's mission. If Randall continues to fail the students' needs, teachers like Juana and Laura will burn out. The school needs to reform/restructure with the community's changing needs. The institution of school is to serve the population. This school is currently in a bilingual environment, therefore should work for it, not against it. . . . The fact that the principal wants to address these issues is a good sign, hopefully with the understanding that this kind of transformation will take time, detailed thought and a school wide focused goal. This type of needed reform would not occur in a weekend inservice. A school/ community-wide vision needs to be developed and outlined over time. The support and energy needs to be school/community wide in order to be successful for all participants.

—Teacher Working on ESL Certification

The process of developing a school-wide vision must be an ongoing process and cannot become personal. The entire staff must agree to be open and honest with each other and must realize they are there for the children. Being afraid of the unknown is common, but once the bridge has begun to be built all staff and children can be supported in who they are and who they are trying to become.

—Teacher

This, of course, also depends upon the principal's effectiveness in leading the staff through a consensus building process, a means by which decisions are made through mutual agreement and compromise, not through voting. Decisions should not be imposed, but should be continually referenced from an established vision and program. Unfortunately, it sounds as though the principal has not educated himself and he may not prove to be an effective leader in the process. He too, must engage in the process of learning and/or hire a facilitator who can guide the school through the process of establishing a vision until he has some facility with and grasp of the issues.

. . . In order to work successfully with the changing demographics at Randall School, the ability to discuss issues openly and honestly must first be developed. This requires that the principal foster an atmosphere of trust, in which in-depth exploration of the issues can take place. It is clear from the case study that most of the teachers are aware of the need for change, but have had no means to open the discussion among themselves. Fear and insecurity have made dialogue nearly impossible. Given the magnitude of the changes required, it is not surprising that there would be fear and distrust, particularly since the school has fostered an autonomous, individualistic style up until now.

—Student in Master's Program

I think that the best way that we can respond to your concerns is by using this time during the retreat to allow the school staff an opportunity to articulate and share their beliefs about students, schooling, and the social issues that impact our school. Of course, we must first set up a guideline of norms that we will agree to adhere to throughout this discussion, such as respect for others' views and opinions, allowing others to come to closure when expressing themselves, etc. Some of the questions which we could address include the following: Do we really hold the view that all students can learn and that they can all achieve to high standards? What are our beliefs regarding bilingual education and effective English instruction for second language learners? I think that it is important to extend this discussion to include paraprofessionals as well as active family members. It is important to recognize that if we are going to alter the school's curriculum style to better serve second language learners, then we must take the time and energy to create a model that is inclusive and supported by all members of the school staff, and not just one grade level or a few teachers. Through this dialogue we can then eventually come up with a vision statement regarding our view on how to best serve all of the students in our school and particularly second language learners.

—First Year Teacher

Shared Responsibility

Respondents felt that responsibility for students' success should be equitably distributed among all staff at Randall. A school-wide approach would ensure that the sole burden of the academic success of English language learners would not fall to just a few teachers.

Three teachers cannot be responsible for educating the growing numbers of linguistically diverse students. Laura and Juana are setting a good example for the staff by team teaching. Although they are aware they will have to compromise the way they each do things, they are willing to pool their resources in order to create a more appropriate learning environment. A school committed to acting as a community and valuing its resources will be inviting for families and students. Success will be more easily achieved.

—Prospective Teacher

It appears that because there are only three bilingual teachers who **alone address every issue** concerning second language learners the rest of the staff at Randall have begun to form opinions and criticisms about second language learners and learning in general. This happens because the organization itself creates a sort of 'divisiveness' thus also creating misinformed assumptions about second language learners. By recognizing a need for change in the existing structure of the school, then an educational belief like Laura's and others can be openly shared.

—Graduate Student

ESL teachers are expected to teach English at a breakneck speed, provide meaningful content-area instruction in all subject areas, solve all problems of limited-English proficient students, and serve as mediating link between home and school. In other words, ESL staff at Randall Elementary meet with more challenges than regular classroom teachers. Somewhere, in between the ideal vision and the complicated school world of proposals and administrative plans, teachers have to deal with day-to-day working relationships with the group of students who have been assigned to them. Therefore, all teachers in the school need to establish a common vision for the school and programs, and work towards a common goal as a community.

—Teacher

Before doing team teaching with just one teacher in the school, I would tell her that changes must be done as a whole. The population in the whole school has changed and there should be a consensus with every staff member to make big changes. Children can not be served in only one classroom or grade, there must be a consistent program to see results.

—Elementary Bilingual Teacher

Team Teaching

Collaboration is an essential component of a total school approach. Team teaching as an organizational structure assumes collaboration and cooperation and shared responsibility for students. Respondents had both praise for team teaching and cautions about its implementation. Many directly addressed the loss of autonomy that can occur in a team teaching situation and the great possibility for small misunderstandings to develop into larger problems without strong communication. Several respondents caution that without a school wide plan, teaming will be an ineffective solution to the problems at Randall.

It is best to talk about the concerns and thoughts you are feeling with your team prior to making the commitment. Laura, you have already accepted to team teach with Juana, and this problem will only be enhanced if you do not develop an understanding for each other's concerns and positions on these major educational issues. Granted, you have never had to teach second language learners, but you do have some experience in ESL second language acquisition as a good start. . . . As for the loss of freedom in the classroom, it is not the end of the world. You must see that the overall effort is to improve the general academic success of second language learners and not solely maintaining a personal freedom. Rather, you will find yourself feeling fortunate to have a team you can count on for moral support and planning efforts. Furthermore, you do not live in a microcosm of a world, where each classroom is its own entity. You do bear the same responsibility as the bilingual teacher for helping educate the students you teach and help them attain the academic levels of success in English as well, and this means changing your perspective.

—Bilingual Teacher–Spanish Component

Laura's sense of enjoyment on having freedom to teach in her own class-room is a real big issue with all teachers. This is quite understandable, as teachers feel more "secure" when they don't feel everyone's eyes on their teaching. The worst fear for many teachers is criticism from peers. On top of all this also the issue of teaching differently because of the bilingual component. Who is going to be helping or criticizing her teaching ability if not another teacher and that teacher is a "bilingual" teacher? Also Laura's feelings regarding Juana's relationship as a teacher are very real and scary. Many teachers who are actually very good friends of mine, I would *never* want to team teach with them for the same reasons that Laura stated, not getting along, ways of organizing instruction, goals for students, classroom organization and for me, methods of discipline weren't compatible.

—Bilingual Teacher

Personally I feel there is much more to be gained than lost by teaming. However, I acknowledge that autonomy is valuable. It does give you a lot of freedom. But again, she must consider the needs of their students over her own temporary discomfort. So in order to make the transition easier for Laura, maybe she and Juana could begin by teaming in just one or two subjects. That way they could get used to the process of working together and work out the kinks before plunging into a full teaming situation. The other thing Laura should make sure to do is talk with Juana about their approaches to organizing instruction and classroom management before the school year begins so that they can come up with a consensus on approaches they can both comfortably live with. With that agreement in place, they can be free to focus on the content and methods of their instruction during the school year.

—Teacher with several years experience in a teaming situation

I would tell Laura that if she is going to team teach, she would have to teach the English part of the teaming, and she does not need to know the other language (Spanish). She needs to teach content in English, using strategies for second language learners, she has to teach ESL, and she needs to teach Language Arts for her students who speak English as first language. She can start implementing what she learned in her ESL class with her second language learners. I would tell Laura that I am sure that Juana would be very willing to help her with the culture and needs of the Latino children.

—Bilingual Teacher

Laura is justified in her hesitation to enter into such a new style of teaching. Her fears, such as losing instructional freedom and having goals, styles, organization, and discipline that are different are real issues that need to be carefully considered. Before agreeing to team teach with Juana I would recommend that the two teachers discuss their philosophies and practices in these areas. Other areas that should be discussed are the specific roles they hope to play in the teaming relationship along with their goals for the students.

—Graduate Student

Finally I would recommend to Laura that she and Juana make a clear plan for instruction. They should address the following questions:

How much Spanish will the English speakers be taught? That is, is it a two-way bilingual program?

How much time will be spent each day in the second language?

What will be taught in the second language—content? Games? Random vocabulary?

Will they use the Concept Development Strategy (Miramontes, Nadeau, & Commins, 1997) with concept comprehension lessons, integrated group, and scaffolded oral expression?

How will literacy be taught? Will English speakers be introduced to Spanish reading?

When will Spanish speakers be introduced to English reading?

How will they designate Spanish and English environments?

How will it be decided which language will be considered the primary language?

When, if at all, will students be transitioned into an all-English reading and speaking environment?

—Teacher

READER REACTIONS TO "FRIENDSHIP, PROFESSIONALISM, AND PROGRAMS"

SUMMARY AND ADDITIONAL QUESTIONS

This case raises many issues for teachers who may need to adapt their instructional approaches to accommodate changing demographics. These changes are especially challenging when the makeup of the student population is no longer mirrored in the teaching staff. For many teachers who have experienced years of teaching in communities where the students are from similar backgrounds as them, the appearance of students from different ethnic, cultural, and linguistic backgrounds can produce much trepidation and discomfort.

Lack of familiarity with students' cultures and backgrounds can cause people to feel defensive. Insecurity about not speaking the language of the students can lead teachers to feel they can't or shouldn't or don't need to play a role in their education. It is easy for schools to become fractionalized with certain students relegated to a certain set of teachers who are seen as having the obligation to meet the specialized needs of this group. Teaching staffs often descend into an "us and them" mentality that divides them around whose job it is to make sure students learn English and achieve academic success.

Despite these tensions and challenges most teachers want to do the best job they possibly can for the students they teach. This care for the well-being of the students will often prompt teachers to try to make changes, even knowing that controversy and alienation among their peers may result. They are to be commended. Some specific questions to continue to consider in relation to this case are:

- What kind of staff development is needed in order for all teachers to feel confident in teaching linguistically diverse populations?
- What is the rationale for primary language use and how can limited resources in the students' primary language be used to their greatest effect?
- How and to what extent should teachers take steps on their own to solve problems that arise from the way resources are organized in their school?
- What is the role of the principal and other building leaders in orchestrating a school wide vision and creating a culture of collaboration?
- How can schools teachers participate in the work of creating a school wide plan?

- At what point does "going along with the school-wide program" infringe upon individual teachers' academic freedom and their ability to personalize instruction?
- What obligation (if any) does a teacher have to promote equitable contributions by all colleagues?
- How does race/language affect collegial relationships? What is the role of the majority culture/language teacher within a diverse staff?

INTRODUCTION TO CASE 4

The final case in this book explores issues related to standards and assessment and their implementation in linguistically diverse settings. The case describes the situation of Andrew, an experienced teacher who has volunteered to participate in his district's efforts to delineate standards to guide instruction. In this process he encounters unexpected hurdles in trying to account for his second language learners.

Among the questions raised in this case are the following: How does the presence of second language learners affect the kind of assessment system that must be in place within a school? How can the achievement of second language learners be measured accurately? How should and how does assessment impact instruction? How do legislative mandates regarding assessment and accountability interface with the reality and needs of linguistically diverse classrooms and schools?

CASE 4: "WHAT IS EQUAL TREATMENT?"

Andrew has been teaching third grade for 15 years at Edgeview Elementary, a large school (600+ students) in a middle sized city in the Northeast. Edgeview was the district's first "ESL center school." For as long as Andrew has been there it has served second language learners of English—just a few in his first years—about 30% of the student body now. As with other schools in his district, not only have the numbers grown in the past several years there are also some demographic changes with the new arrivals. These new arrivals' literacy and academic skills represent a wider range in their first languages than previous students. Andrew was reminded of the school's progress and history as he went from Tatiana, his recent Russian arrival, to Dom Toc his new Indonesian student, and then to Maria the daughter of a Mexican migrant worker.

There are so many languages represented at Edgeview that it hasn't been feasible to implement a bilingual program. They have stayed with all-English instruction although the school has hired a few native language assistants to help out with home school communications and an initial "welcome to the school" program for entering English language learners. There are four full-time certified ESL teachers assigned to the building this year, the most support the school has ever received.

For the staff at Edgeview, accommodating the needs of English language learners has become a routine part of the school's planning. As the numbers of these students have grown, the school has changed in many ways and the program has evolved considerably. When Andrew goes to district-level meetings or sees teachers from other schools on the weekends, he realizes how far Edgeview has come in meeting the needs of students. When he began the ESL program was delivered by noncertified instructional aides who worked one on one with students in the back of the classroom. Without a defined curriculum or ESL series, the aides focused on basic vocabulary and usually just helped students to finish their assignments. About 10 years ago, as numbers began to rise, the aides were trained to provide more formal oral language instruction for 45 minutes a day in a pullout program. They taught in small groups using a grammar-based ESL series adopted by the district.

Things stayed that way for about 4 years until they realized that students needed a stronger program. As a result, the district began to hire certified ESL teachers instead of instructional aides and tutors, and the focus of ESL shifted towards formal literacy development. The ESL continuum that had been created to document growth in English, had originally focused solely on listening and speaking skills, now it was expanded to include reading and writing indicators. Also ESL instructional time was increased from 45 minutes a day to 60–75 minutes.

When the school implemented extended blocks for reading and writing they also developed a master schedule that coordinated ESL with literacy. So instead of pulling out students whenever it seemed convenient for the classroom teacher, they now coordinated the student's instruction in English as a second language with their literacy work. Now, all faculty have received basic training in second language acquisition and ESL teachers have been included in all the professional development opportunities related to literacy instruction. The staff even convinced the district to allow a once-a-week delayed start of 90 minutes so that classroom and support personnel can have joint planning time.

Andrew had nearly forgotten the bitterness that used to divide the faculty. In his early years, one of the most contentious issues that faced the staff was over how to distribute the second language learners among the classrooms. He was reminded of this when he ran into Sally, who teaches at one of the many schools in the district that are just beginning to experience the linguistic diversity that Edgeview has always known. Sally wanted to know Andrew's opinion of "clustering" versus "scattering" students.

Andrew remembered when district administrators suggested that instead of scattering the ESL students across all the classrooms at each grade level, that they be clustered in only one or two classrooms. The faculty was told that the students would not feel as isolated and the teachers would have reasonable numbers to facilitate small group teaching. Many teachers at Edgeview had initially resisted clustering. He can still picture his colleague Francine standing up at a faculty meeting and complaining that she didn't think it was fair to take the diversity away from her other students. She talked about all the opportunities for multicultural enrichment that were provided by having an ESL student in her class and how much she would miss that if clustering were to happen.

With lots of grumbling they tried clustering and sure enough students became more confident in their interactions and it was much easier to accommodate their needs with a "critical mass." Now there are so many second language learners at Edgeview that everyone has many ESL students—often from several different language groups—in their homeroom. This year Andrew has a class of 27, 8 of whom are English language learners.

Andrew assured his friend that they would probably resolve this issue as they did at Edgeview. With every change they have seen students make more progress. The academic expectations the staff holds for English language learners are much higher than they've ever been and he's learned that every time the faculty increases expectations, the students respond. But he also knows there are new challenges ahead.

One thing bothering him is that despite providing more focused literacy instruction, he's never sure that he's doing enough or that the students are getting the kind of support that they need. His concerns have increased since the state instituted mandatory standards testing in reading and writing.

Schools across the state are now graded based on the results of the mandated reading and writing and math tests. Every school's scores are reported in the newspapers. For 3 years in a row, Edgeview has been in the bottom one half of the district. This really frustrates teachers who believe they are trying their hardest. Many feel its unfair to compare schools this way since different schools serve very different populations and schools like Edgeview that serve many second language learners seem unfairly penalized. They are angered by the attitude expressed in the community that the second language learners are bringing down the scores for the whole school.

At the last PTO meeting, several parents, pointing to Edgeview's scores in the paper, threatened to remove their children from the school. They wanted to be assured that their children weren't suffering from lowered expectations. When they were shown the scores broken out by sub groups, they could see that native English speakers were performing at the same level or above as their peers in schools with few second language learners. What they couldn't see was the progress of the second language learners.

The real problem from Andrew's point of view is that the tests, which are designed for native English speakers, do not really measure the growth that students have made. Every year, he has had students enter his third grade class with no English skills and in many cases very little literacy in their home language. By the end of the year, they are speaking basic conversational English and are reading and writing about familiar topics, but they aren't ready for the state test. If they don't take the test they are counted as zeros. When they do, the progress they have made is invisible and, therefore, overlooked. The math test poses other problems, lots of his students are very strong in computation, but there are so many word problems on the test it seems to be measuring their English reading rather than their math skills.

His feelings on the subject have intensified since he began to participate in a district committee that is developing progress indicators or benchmarks for the elementary content standards. Andrew is on the task force working on the language arts standards. Committee members have attended a series of professional development inservices on standards-based teaching. Training sessions have emphasized how instruction should be guided by a clear vision of what students are supposed to know and be able to do. In a standards based system teachers are supposed to differentiate the delivery of instruction to meet the range of student background knowledge and abilities. He has also learned that assessments should drive instruction—that you have to know what students already know and then document what they learn as a result of instruction.

Andrew is excited by the idea of looking at his teaching through the standards lens. He feels that it is, in part, an answer to his concerns about documenting academic progress for English second language learners. He is particularly interested in the idea of assessment driving instruction and the need for benchmarks of progress along the road to standards. Other teachers at Edgeview are also excited by the idea that the growth indicators could be developed. One teacher has even begun to talk about how the report cards could be changed to reflect student's actual progress.

Although his colleagues at school are supportive, Andrew feels he's facing an uphill battle with members of the standards committee. Most of them come from schools with few second language learners and don't understand either the process of second language development or how limiting the current assessments are in documenting students' growth. Andrew is convinced that as they are developing the benchmarks for the language arts standards they should include progress indicators for second language learners. With a wider range of assessments and ways of determining what it is that students do know it would be possible to document the actual growth that the English language learners are making.

He was surprised at the amount of resistance to his suggestion when he brought this up at the previous committee work session. Several people said that having these kinds of extended indicators would weaken the standards rather than providing a more detailed road map for how students are progressing toward them. A couple of key members on the committee are from schools with only a few second language learners. They suggested that a separate set of standards should be developed for the ESL teachers to use in their classes. Andrew disagrees with them and is frustrated that they don't seem to understand that the indicators they have been using as models were developed based on the performance of native speakers. He tried to explain how they assume a certain level of exposure and language development experience to begin with. Second language learners start in a different place in English. The problem teachers have faced at Edgeview is precisely that current assessments don't measure the progress they make just to get to the point where the native English speakers are beginning with all their English language experience.

He is convinced that English language learners' needs should be central to the work they are doing. Because the standards are supposed to be for all students, he thinks that the benchmarks they are developing should be broad enough to document the progress of every student. Although it may be that some teachers on the committee still don't have a lot of second language learners Andrew feels strongly about representing the interests of the teachers in his school. He knows that they are counting on the district to provide them with the support they need to document the growth that all students are making. To begin the benchmarks at the place where native English speakers are in their language development is to ignore huge amounts of growth that the second language learners make on their road to the standards. It also says that the needs of second language learners are not everybody's responsibility.

Andrew knows he needs to speak up again. This afternoon, the language arts subcommittee is having their second meeting to actually work on the benchmarks. He wonders how he can help his committee to understand how language and literacy development of all students should be reflected in the standards. He wonders what he can do to help them see his point of view.

READER REACTIONS TO ANDREW'S SITUATION

REACTIONS TO "WHAT IS EQUAL TREATMENT?"

Several themes already addressed in previous cases re-emerged in response to Andrew's dilemma. They include the reality of the changing demographics, the challenge of adapting to these changes and providing instruction matched to the needs of students. Respondents also returned to the issue of individual teachers' responsibility to initiate or push for changes in a sometimes unsupportive environment. Themes unique to this case revolve around the challenges of accountability in linguistically diverse settings.

Andrew's Reality: Same or Different Than Mine

The differing reactions of respondents to Andrew's situation reflect the differences in the ways that schools currently address linguistic diversity. Schools vary greatly in where they are in the demographic shift occurring across the country. They also differ in their level of awareness, understanding, and acceptance of these population changes in their school community. Some respondents easily saw themselves and their schools reflected in the description of Edgeview. Others were shocked at the resources and degree of support that existed there, especially given the reality of their own settings.

> Andrew's story parallels my teaching experience in several ways. First of all, I have been teaching eighteen years and have seen the progression of servicing the needs of the Second Language Learner. Placement of ESL students was also a big dilemma for our school at the time. "Clustering" versus "scattering" students was never really discussed for placement. The ESL students would be placed into classes at random, not really considering their language needs. Some teachers would be more willing to be patient and work with the ESL students in the class, therefore receiving more ESL students. On the other hand, other teachers would tend to ignore them until they could speak English, which of course was a very ineffective strategy.
> —Elementary Teacher

> This case study seemed like it took place within a typical school in my district. We serve many ESL children and their non-English speaking families. Yet there are a few employees in the district, especially in the administration who don't have any knowledge about educating English language learners. They have little insight into the realities of life in a school and its classrooms where 40% of the population is Spanish-speaking.
> —Elementary Teacher

I feel that Andrew is lucky to work at Edgeview because the school has a lot of positive programs and teachers for the most part. It's amazing that for 600+ students there are four full-time certified ESL teachers, amazing! I think about [my district's] two middle schools with the same population, but with 40–60% of the population being second language learners. Our middle schools only have one full time ESL teacher and maybe one or two paraprofessionals to help. Our elementary schools only have paraprofessionals servicing the students along with the bilingual teachers.

—Middle School Teacher

I know that my district would never hire an aide to match each student's language that came into the school that year. We are lucky if we can even get translators at conferences!

—Elementary Teacher

School Structure, Planning, Collaboration, and Professional Development

Whether or not Andrew's reality reflected their own, many readers pointed to the particular strengths of Edgeview's organizational structure and its use of resources. The feature most often noted was the built in common planning time provided to allow cross-teacher coordination.

Basically, I saw many positives for all students at this school: the correlated ESL and Literacy instruction, the weekly planning time for the staff, the clustering of ESL students and the high expectations placed on second language learners are all strengths of the program.

—Elementary Bilingual Teacher

The case presents an idealistic view of reality. Having access to the supply of ESL training, the number of ESL teachers and the coordination of the literacy block schedule incorporated with ESL instruction—not as a pullout facet would be amazing. I'd love to see how the faculty went about structuring and implementing a schedule that could accommodate *all* second language learners during the literacy block.

—Master's Candidate

I really liked the idea of a late start to give common planning times to grade levels. In elementary school, that's a problem. Grade levels do not always, and sometimes never, have common planning time let alone support staff available during your planning time. My school has what we call Standardized Day in which the students are dismissed at 1:30 rather than 2:45. This time is allocated for staff development activities, but sometimes it is grade level and specialist planning time.

—Elementary Teacher

I also liked the idea of the time set aside for planning between classroom teachers and joint personnel. Coordination between ESL teachers and classroom teachers is essential, but nonexistent at my school. I know that if there was more cohesion between the ESL and regular classrooms in terms of units and content area lessons that the ESL children would benefit much more from their instruction. What they would be learning would be reinforced as they moved between the classrooms and they would hear vocabulary and concepts over and over again. Think how preferable this is to learning two separate concepts each day as they go between classrooms!

—Elementary Teacher

I truly feel that most of the problem is that teachers do not have enough time in the day to get everything done. I personally take homework with me to be graded or recorded in the gradebook. Teachers have families and other obligations and finding time that an ESL teacher and classroom teacher can meet can be very difficult. I have struggled with setting up times with the special needs students and their supportive staff. It is exciting to know that a district is finally seeing the need for ESL students and the planning that goes along with it.

—Third Grade Teacher

Standards: How Best to Integrate Second Language Learners

The issue of standards and how they should be applied to second language learners drew a variety of responses from the readers. None advocated abandoning standards for second language learners, but many felt that there should be separate standards and benchmarks for ELLs. These disagreements reflected to some extent a lack of common vocabulary regarding the differences between standards—what we want students to know; benchmarks—indicators of how students can demonstrate their knowledge and skills; and assessments—instruments and tasks used to measure their progress. Responses reflected differing interpretations of what it means to treat all students "equally" and/or "equitably," to "hold high expectations" for learners or even what it means to "speak English."

The benchmarks should not be modified or lowered to meet the needs of second language learners. All students should be held accountable for achieving high standards. It is the school's responsibility to determine how to best meet the needs of these students. Schools must determine what it will take to enable them to meet these standards. If benchmarks are changed it will lead to lower standards for all students. Schools need to be held accountable for high student achievement. Schools should examine research and use best practices to help students become proficient readers and writers. Teachers need to have high expectations for all students including second language learners.

—Prospective Teacher

As a classroom teacher, I believe that standards are a useful and necessary evil. Our children are growing up in a society that is technologically advancing at a speed that most adults cannot comprehend. These children will have to compete economically in a work force that becomes more divided according to class and ability. I want nothing more than to be able to provide the skills and knowledge that all of my students will need to be successful.

—Elementary Teacher

There doesn't necessarily need to be two sets of standards, in fact, this would only lead to confusion and dispute over which standards should be applied to each child. The standards and benchmarks only need to be written in a broad enough way, so that they can document the growth of ALL learners.

—Elementary Bilingual Teacher

Standards created for native English learners are not equitable for English Language Learners. They do not take into account their unique struggles and the different strides ESL students must take in order to meet the prescribed goals. Amended standards that account for English Language Learners' journeys will accurately depict their progress. Currently, teachers do not have equal assessment standards for this population. It seems only constitutional that these children be given standards that accurately measure their progress, so they are not held to the accomplishments of a very different population. At the same they should be held to high standards and expected to eventually reach similar goals as native English learners.

—Prospective Teacher

Teachers need to be accountable for providing the students with a quality education that strives for the benchmarks. . . . A working portfolio that reflects growth in the area of language will coincide well with benchmarks. Development towards those benchmarks is what teachers and ESL teachers should strive for with careful observations and assessments. I don't feel it would be beneficial to have a second set of standards for the ESL students, but providing teachers with growth [indicators] should be sufficient to help with literacy development in the new language.

—Prospective Teacher

As our local school districts, our state legislature and our federal government keep working to create assessments for our students, schools, and the public education system, the way the assessments meet the needs of all students will become a larger and larger issue. Students who are second language learners need to be assessed and held accountable to standards that are adapted for their needs, Just as we make accommodations for students who are classified as specialized learners with disabilities, we should also make accommodations for the specialized language learners. In order to make this happen, it is important for teachers like Andrew to speak their mind and create representation for second language learners because the advocates for this population of students are not yet strong in number.

—Prospective Teacher

Creating a curriculum that serves ESL students is key. The goal of the ESL program should be to eventually align completely with the regular grade level expectations for language arts. While learning English, the ESL students should not be exempted from benchmarks; however, the expectations and qualifiers should be personalized to the ESL students' needs and abilities. Designing a curriculum with benchmarks and qualifiers that are accessible to ESL students will help develop English abilities so that the ESL students are ready to transition into the standard language arts curriculum. ESL students' progress should be measured positively in terms of growth and not negatively in regard to deficiencies.

—Prospective Teacher

Andrew needs to convince the standards committee that viewing standards as a series of benchmarks to mark progress is not a dilution of standards. Students still have their academic benchmarks, and their progress will be documented and proven as necessary. What needs to become the primary focus now is a system that works in the best interest of all students.

—Prospective Teacher

This is another area in which all staff members must take a vested interest, because we are all responsible for the education of these children. They are no longer an isolated group sent to the basement or segregated to one class-room. They are a vital part of the student body and their language needs need to be recognized and included as a part of their standards. That does not mean lower expectations or drastic changes in content, but it does re-quire a change in attitude and curricular adaptations that are parallel to the English curriculum.

—Elementary Teacher

Is This Appropriate Testing for Second Language Learners?

Educational institutions are increasingly being held accountable for the academic achievement of their students (No Child Left Behind, 2002). The pressures embodied in federal and state mandates are felt more strongly in schools with large numbers of second language learners. In these schools the normal variability that exists among students is greatly extended by the range of students' proficiency and academic background in their first language, as well as the length of time they have been learning English. As districts seek ways to easily and economically measure the progress of their students, instruments designed for one purpose may be being used for another, whether or not they are appropriate to that task.

With the demands being made by state institutions in the name of account-ability and productivity, a vital piece of the puzzle has not been considered: test validity. It is a piece of the puzzle that is obvious to those who work di-rectly with second language learners, but is not so obvious to those in poli-tics. The reason this piece has been missing in so many discussions, I think, is that district officials, social scientists, and government workers often ar-gue that "everyone is equal here, and therefore everything should be the same when it comes to being accountable." It is an incorrect and erroneous assumption they work under when they consider second language learners to be the same as native English students, except that they "just need to hurry up and catch up." . . . Valid testing is all that anyone really wants, and a sense of accountability from the schools. Those seem reasonable enough to me. It just seems that the demand for accountability has pushed aside concerns for a valid instrument, and a one-size-fits-all attitude has come to dominate public and political conversations.

—Bilingual Teacher–English Component

Few of the assessments that are currently available have been designed to measure the academic progress of ELLs. As a result these students are generally being tested with measures that were designed for native English speakers who have received all of their schooling in English. Many respondents discussed the inherent unfairness of measuring students who were just recently learning English with the same measures used to assess students who had used English for their entire lives.

> Effective education occurs when the needs of all the students are met and when their progress can be demonstrated through formal and informal assessment. The benchmarks have traditionally been based on what was believed to be adequate progress for students speaking only English. Those students started their education in English, progressed through the grade levels in English, lived in their English-speaking communities, and were able to receive all the services necessary in English. This scenario has drastically changed. Not only have expectations for students had to increase according to a rapidly advancing economy, but the public schools have been inundated by families struggling to get a piece of the American Dream.
>
> —Teacher

> The reality is that in far too many schools there are legions of men and women who dedicate their heart and soul's worth of energy day in and day out to provide the best possible learning experiences for their students. And from these efforts, the politicians create *one* measure to ascertain success versus failure. . . . It is not acknowledged that through this type of assessment, children are being compared to one another without any regard to native language factors/experiences. In other words, we are comparing apples and oranges and assuming them to be the same by comparing the "achievement" of second language learners who have been learning English for a limited time, to children who have been exposed and immersed in English for their whole lives. In addition, we are measuring their proficiency in math when the majority of the problems are *word problems*, which wind up assessing language proficiency versus skills of numeracy. Hmmm.
>
> —Master's Candidate

> The assessments that are designed to assess achievement by native English speakers . . . don't take into account special differences unique to ELLs, and make their success on such assessments, quite limited. It is the egalitarian principle of our country extended in a most ridiculous way, with the result that calling a standardized assessment (administered in English) not valid for second language learners is akin to saying "It's because those ELLs

can't learn like the rest of us," a statement no one would sanely support. Politics have intruded into the realm of standardized assessment, where it has no place at all except for to muck up things.

—Bilingual Teacher

It is important to note that if the assessment is in a language in which the students are not proficient, the assessment is really assessing the students' language proficiency, not their knowledge of subject matter.

—Doctoral Student

This measure, specifically the standardized test, is culturally biased. The questions are aimed at tapping into the experiences of Anglo-European students from the upper to middle class. There are no multicultural dimensions to the test that recognize learning styles, experiences, or native languages of second language learners. Nor do these tests accurately reflect the level of growth that a child coming into an all-English environment speaking another language has made. Instead, the child is marked as having further deficits in learning.

—Master's Candidate

In the case of Spanish speaking students, who are becoming more of a majority than a minority, students could take tests in Spanish if they are learning in their first language at a bilingual school. The measurement is of students' ability to think, not in which language they think. If the goal is to only see how everyone in the U.S. speaks, thinks and responds in English, then perhaps an English test is all that should be used. Ultimately, if all students are expected to exit high school as thinking individuals that are academically successful and well rounded shouldn't we assess them from all different angles?

—Art Teacher

Use of Scores Unfair

The use of students' scores to grade and compare schools was found by some respondents to be even more problematic than the testing itself. Federal and state guidelines have come to rely on a system where students, teachers and schools are graded based on the number and percent of students who meet a certain level on either standards-based or standardized tests. The publication of test scores in local newspapers has mushroomed in the past several years as part of a move to keep the public informed.

Many respondents felt that by not accounting for the differences among students when they arrive, these report cards do not provide a picture of students' actual progress nor the effectiveness of teachers and schools in serving them.

> When the reputation and effectiveness of a school is measured by scores from standardized testing, schools with high immigrant and/or non-English speaking populations are at a huge disadvantage.
>
> —Prospective Teacher

> I too am angered. Not at the tests themselves, but at the way they are used. Community members and parents don't understand what the tests show, or better yet, what they don't show. They don't show progress of individuals. They compare students and schools regardless of ethnicity, race, home language, or social class.
>
> —Bilingual Teacher

> My field experience was in a middle school that scored the lowest in [the state] on the standardized testing. These results were published in the paper, and it was very frustrating to both the staff and the students. Students were demoralized, and the staff was very angry and felt penalized. It was disheartening to see, as I knew this staff was as talented and committed as any other staff. I would venture to say they were even more committed, for they were fighting an uphill battle and they knew it! It's frustrating to see such wonderful teachers publicly humiliated because they choose to work with the students that need them the most.
>
> —Prospective Teacher

> The whole idea of giving schools report cards would demolish our public education system. If you look closely at background situations of most schools, the lower economic schools tend to score lower because parental support for education is not there, or you have families that are struggling to make a living and tend to let the school worry about the education of their children. I only wish our legislators and our Governor would come and sit in our classrooms and deal with the issues we deal with every day and try and get them ready for standardized tests with little to no resources.
>
> —Teacher

The first issue to address here is that the standards in and of themselves are useful tools for assessing learning progress as well as driving future instruction. However, by coupling state standards and test scores, and then liking them to *grades for schools*, we are creating a system that is doomed for failure.

—Master's Candidate

Ideal: An Equitable System Would Document Growth

In the view of many of the respondents, a fair and equitable system for accountability would look quite different than the one described in this case. They suggested that given the socioeconomic, cultural, and linguistic variables impacting public schools, judgements of merit should include indicators of how students have grown in their academic abilities. In an ideal system, schools would be credited with and rewarded for the amount of growth their students make.

> The fact that a second language learner is not on grade level is not as serious as a primary language learner because they are starting so much farther behind. The benchmarks need to show growth from non-English speakers to English speakers and readers. These learners are starting a lot lower on the ladder than the other students and it isn't fair to start the judging half way up. . . . The committee needs to understand what we are doing to second language learners by not acknowledging the growth they have made. These children have a huge mountain in front of them. If we do not acknowledge the growth they have made and let them feel successful, why should they try? Possibly Andrew could bring in some examples of work his second language learners have done throughout the year. Illustrate to the committee where his students begin and where they end up. This could show the committee that while they may not be reading and writing at the same level as his other students, they have still made a lot of growth over the year.
>
> —Graduate Student

> Andrew has got to make the point to his colleagues that the point of education is student progress, not just meeting the standards. While standards provide great goals for students, their growth is the most important objective. He might reinforce this idea by presenting the case of a gifted student that comes into third grade already meeting or exceeding the standards. Would this student's teacher be content with his abilities as they are and not worry about challenging him. No, because the goal of education is that students improve in their academic each and every year, regardless of the abilities that they come into the year with.
>
> —Prospective Teacher

Change and the Resistance to It: A Recurring Theme

The kind of accountability system proposed by many of the respondents to the case would require dramatic changes in the ways that schools instruct and assess their students. In this case, as in the previous three, the theme of change, the resistance to change and the level of an individual educator's individual responsibility to act surfaced as important to the readers.

[My school] is in the midst of adding a bilingual strand and it is causing rifts within the professional staff. I think that many teachers are simply afraid of change because of what it may mean; changing their teaching style, investing more time, requiring them to learn new methods and skills, and they may simply be burned-out on teaching. Many of the issues that cause change to be challenging are valid, but if a teacher truly wants to meet the needs of their student population more time and effort must be invested. . . . Change cannot help unless every person—professional and regular staff—is willing to work with their colleagues and is willing to take an active role in the changes that must happen. . . . I believe that many teachers may be opposed to the changes that need to occur to meet the ESL students' needs because they do not understand the methodology and reasoning behind the modifications needed for ESL students.

—Teacher in a highly impacted school

Unfortunately, what Andrew is experiencing is not limited to his school district. This way of thinking is prevalent throughout the country, in every district and in every state. Teachers who work with second language learners need to pick and choose their battles. If all battles are made to be equally important, then all battles may be poorly fought, and not won. . . . Andrew can win this battle, just not in the way he would like. The battle should not be against the ignorant teachers, but should be for his second language students first and foremost.

—Teacher working on ESL certification

There always seems to be resistance when it comes to change. I recommend trying to stay upbeat, yet voice your opinions and expertise. It's thanks to people like Andrew that policies change for better, or for the worse if you do not give your input. Andrew definitely needs to speak up, maybe he needs support from his school so that he is not the only one who does so. Often, people in numbers seem to have an impact on others, whereas one is shoved aside. I believe he should go to his school's administrator, or principal, with this concern.

—Middle School Teacher

In their suggestions for responding to change, many readers touched upon the central theme of this book and this series—reflective practice. For real change to happen reflection must occur along multiple dimensions and at every level of the system. The most immediate concern for most teachers centers on their own teaching. Several readers suggested that good teachers are never satisfied with their instruction and are always seeking to improve themselves.

[In response to] Andrew's remark "Is he doing enough or that the students are getting the kind of support that they need?" I think every 'good' teacher worries about this and is always trying to do more. It once again leads back to time of which there is never enough. I feel that a teacher who is asking themselves these questions and evaluating what is going on in the classroom, is putting the students' needs first.

—Teacher

Another thing that Andrew mentions is even though Edgeview has made a lot of great changes, he is not sure if he is meeting his ESL students' need. Good! I think that as a teacher you should never feel you have reached a point where you no longer have to think about and modify your instruction. Of course, as an educator you should take time to pat yourself on the back for the good job you are doing, but you shouldn't become satisfied with your instruction. You should feel there is more you can do for your students, if you feel comfortable then you are not meeting their needs.

—First Year Teacher

It may be necessary to orchestrate contexts that will stimulate critical reflection. Several readers suggested that a good stimulus for reflection would be to put teachers into the role of second language learners. They thought this would awaken them to the challenges of learning in a second language, and help sensitize teachers to the complexity of being assessed in a second language.

One of the most effective strategies I've seen is role-playing an English language learner to illustrate how handicapping the language barrier is in a testing situation. He could give a simple math word problem or language arts comprehension question to his committee directly translated from the district's assessment. After practicing saying (in Spanish or Indonesian) "Hi, how are you?" and "What is your name?" and "My name is . . ." he can administer the test in Spanish or Indonesian. The committee can experience the frustration level of a student with beginning conversational skills. Afterwards, the committee can debrief this experience and its relevance as they determine district benchmarks.

—Teacher

Andrew needs to put the committee in the shoes of second language learners. Have one of his former students teach a literacy lesson in his or her first language. Let them understand that for these learners they have more than letter names and sounds to learn. These children have vocabulary and concepts to learn.

—Graduate Student

Andrew should bring to the task force samples of his students' work, showing progress and the differences compared to a native language speaker's learning. Perhaps, as an extreme tactic he could give the task force members a culturally biased test, but one that is biased to another culture other than our own. This could "sensitize" them to the needs of second language learners, and show them that tests don't necessarily tell us what we know.

—Bilingual Teacher

The comments in response to this case once again highlight the complexity of teaching in the face of rapidly changing demographics. They also stress the need for teachers to continually analyze what they are doing and why. For lasting change to occur, reflection and action need to move beyond an individual's classroom to an analysis of how classroom and school practices are linked to broader district policies. Some readers suggested that only an ongoing collaborative process of inquiry could truly provide the kind of support needed to sustain change.

Perhaps Andrew cannot make these changes and be the only voice for what he believes, but he can be the catalyst that motivates other teachers to take action. I think that this issue regarding standards sooner or later—probably sooner—will have to be addressed and hopefully there will be socially active people who take a stance and fight for the ESL students.

—Teacher

[T]here is an attitude pretty firmly ingrained in many educators in schools throughout the country that their business is the business of teaching the same kinds of kids they remember having twenty years ago—kids that spoke English, and whose parents spoke English, too. I feel that if change is to happen, it needs to occur in firmly committed, tightly knit schools that can serve as an example to the rest of the educational community. [T]hose teachers who believe that the kids that don't speak English aren't their problem simply need to retire. There just shouldn't be enough room in the profession for them.

—Third Grade Bilingual Teacher

If this committee is struggling this hard with these ideals then maybe this needs to be a district wide reevaluation of goals and philosophical views. The only way to make change happen is to go to the people who have the influence to change things.

—Prospective Teacher

Even if the committee was not swayed by Andrew's arguments or evidence from Edgeview, his school could continue to gather English acquisition data from student assessments in both languages to help his school design and implement effective programs. This data will also be useful as time passes and other schools in the district face growing numbers of English language learners. Schools experiencing ELL population growth are bound to experience the stressful situation of meeting mandatory testing standards set for native English speakers. Edgeview will have compiled data that will be useful to help other schools and the district see how English acquisition, literacy, and content are concepts progress differently for ELL students while students eventually meet native English speaker standards in the long run.

—Teacher

READER REACTIONS TO
"WHAT IS EQUAL TREATMENT?"

SUMMARY AND ADDITIONAL QUESTIONS

The presence of second language learners of English in schools presents challenges in every aspect of their education. One area that is particularly important is that of assessment. Teachers and schools are expected to be accountable for the academic progress of all of their students. In most cases they still rely on measures that have been developed for native English speakers being taught in all English programs to assess the achievement of second language learners.

Many teachers feel that the kinds of standardized tests that are given to students to rate schools or determine school effectiveness don't really help them in planning for the needs of students—even for native English speakers. The skills are too broadly defined and the test scores come too late to impact their day to day instruction. Additionally they feel that the tests don't reveal the kinds of growth and progress that second language learners do make. Concerns over the dilution of expectations that might be caused by creating special indicators for second language learners have caused many teachers to resist these modifications. Yet, the issue of assessment is a critical one and will need to be continually confronted. With this in mind consider the following questions.

- What kind of assessment practices would present the most accurate picture of students' academic progress?
- What role can and should individual teachers play in the development of assessments?
- Are some instruments better suited to one purpose or another? What happens when a test designed for one purpose is used for a different one?
- What is the source of "cultural bias" in standardized testing and how can its effects be minimized?
- What role does assessment in students' primary language play in documenting academic achievement?
- What kind of professional development is needed to support teachers in their efforts to differentiate instruction and assessment in order for them to meet the full range of linguistic and academic proficiency of their students?

II

PUBLIC ARGUMENTS

As the two previous volumes of this series, *Culture and Teaching* (Liston & Zeichner, 1996) and *Gender and Teaching* (Maher & Ward, 2002) have pointed out, in most democracies education is a publicly funded, state-supported endeavor. As a principal public institution, the nation's schools are at the center of extensive and often strident discourse. Look and listen anywhere—in the articles and editorials of newspapers, on radio talk shows, at school board meetings or business round tables, in the halls of government, in the offices of social service agencies, or even in the aisles of your local supermarket. Everywhere, people come together, public education is the focus of debate and analysis. As teachers, we must be aware of and enter into these discussions wherever they occur. To do so adequately requires that we have informed opinions about the types of claims that are made about students, teachers, and the functions and purposes of education. Unfortunately, teacher education programs typically pay little attention to the external context of schools, although it is clear that they should. This volume, as part of a series on reflective practice, is part of the attempt to put larger societal issues into the core of teacher preparation.

In Part I we presented four case studies that highlight how the increasing linguistic diversity in today's schools poses multiple challenges for educators. On virtually any day of the school year at every grade level, teachers can find themselves facing new arrivals who do not speak English and who may or may not bring prior academic preparation to the classroom.

These students are likely to either be immigrants, the children of immigrants, or the children of temporary visitors. In any given classroom, there may be English language learners who fled their homes in the middle of the night because of war. Others' parents may have brought them here out of a desperate attempt to make a living to feed their family. Still, others may be the children of visiting professors, graduate students, scientists, or engineers. For many of the students, the transitions their families are experiencing often limit the family's financial resources and economic pressures can play a big role in these children's lives.

Much of the public discourse around linguistic diversity centers on whether or not immigrant students are learning English quickly enough under the current system and if not, why not? There is little disagreement that living and prospering in the United States necessitates speaking English well. However, there are many other questions whose answers engender debate. What does it mean to "speak English well"? How well is good enough? How long does it take to become proficient? How do you measure proficiency? What is the best route to developing this proficiency? Is English the sole means for advancement or only part of what is needed to function in a multicultural society?

The case studies demonstrate that the great variation in the composition of individual schools, the circumstances and background of the learners, as well as the preparation of their teachers require that the responses to linguistic diversity be multifaceted. Guidance is needed regarding day to day instructional practice, how to best meet the students' needs through English, the sharing of instructional responsibility, instructional accountability, finding the time and resources to teach students in a language they don't understand, as well as communication with students' families and community. The positions taken to address these challenges ideally should be broad-based and informed by the nature of instruction and what constitutes best classroom practice.

The reality is that almost the entire public debate has been marked by only one aspect of this complex challenge—whether students' primary language should be used in school. This is despite the fact that fewer than a third of students in the United States who speak English as a second language are in programs that provide them any instruction in their first language (Macias, 1997, 1998; Mora, 2003). As demonstrated in the cases, there is a multitude of other concerns facing teachers. Nonetheless, whether or not English should be the sole language of instruction rather than addressing the more complicated issue of what instruction should look like, has been the subject of local and state ballot initiatives that have sought to legislate what languages can and can't be used in public schools. At the time of writing this book initiatives restricting bilingual education had been passed in California, Arizona, and Massachusetts, whereas Colorado voters rejected a similar proposal. Yet in all of these states, the academic achievement of language minority students continues to be problematic.

Federal policies have also influenced decision making around the use of students' primary language in instruction. For example, although the "No Child Left Behind" legislation did not impose restrictions regarding how long a language other than English could be used for instruction and assessment, it did include guidelines for assessing all students in English Language Arts within 3 years of arrival. It did not include any substantial guidelines for how to best meet the needs of second language learners.

The following three public arguments *"English is the Glue that Holds Our Nation Together," "Bilingual Education is a Must"* and *"A Pragmatic Approach"* present the most common reasoning put forth in the debate over how best to educate students in linguistically diverse settings. They reflect deeply held and often unexamined attitudes about the role of immigrants in our society and perceptions of the extent to which the English language is seen as a symbol of unity or a sign of patriotism. The *English is the Glue* and *Bilingual Education is a Must* arguments reflect opposing camps that advocate for and against the use of the primary language in instruction. These positions mirror similar camps described in *Culture and Teaching* (Liston & Zeichner, 1996) that split on incorporating, recognizing, or promoting students' home cultures in instruction. *A Pragmatic Approach*, which shares points of view with each of the other two, also addresses directly the reality of day to day instructional issues.

The expectations each of us hold stem from our beliefs, values, biases, and assumptions (Good & Brophy, 2000). These expectations play a very important role in students' academic success. As a professional educator it is essential that you be able to articulate your beliefs and the understandings upon which they are based, not just to argue in public, but more importantly because these will all translate into your day to day classroom practice. Specifically, in working with linguistic diversity it is important to understand how your beliefs about language acquisition, bilingualism, immigration, and other related issues will influence your decision-making and affect the quality of instruction you provide to second language learners.

Your analysis of and reaction to the public arguments is a fundamental component of reading this book as it will allow you to examine your own expectations and practices. We hope that the examination and discussion of these public arguments will also enable you to make further sense of the claims heard and read about daily, and help you to articulate and understand better your own views. These are complicated issues and it is unlikely that any individual's views will fit neatly into one category or another. It is most likely that you will share ideas and sentiments in each of the arguments and disagree with others. To that end, we encourage you to "enter" into each point of view, understanding it on its own terms and to also look at each one of the arguments with some distance and skepticism.

As you read the public arguments think about how they would translate into practice. Absolutist positions, even those that resonate with your current beliefs, may offer you little in the way of actual guidance for daily instruction. For each argument, examine the kinds of solutions they offer and whether these solutions would provide the kind of flexibility necessary for addressing the complexity of teachers' and students' needs in the classroom.

After each public argument we raise additional general and specific questions and issues. We do not elaborate a lengthy list, but encourage you, especially in your class discussions and analyses, to explore these positions further. We also link the public arguments to the case studies in Part I. We hope that this linkage will enable a further discussion of the particular incidents in Part I and the general claims made in Part II.

ENGLISH IS THE GLUE THAT HOLDS OUR NATION TOGETHER

America is a great country made up of people from many lands. For over 200 years people have been coming to the United States to seek freedom and economic opportunity. To become the nation we are has taken great sacrifices that have in return provided our citizens, old and new alike, the greatest opportunities of any nation on earth. You can arrive poor and uneducated, and within a generation you and your family can prosper in ways unimaginable in the place you left behind.

How has this been possible? What is it that brings us all together? The answer is simple—the commonality of the English language. Our country has embraced wave after wave of immigrants with one simple request. If you want to fully participate in the American Dream, you must learn English. For generations, immigrants have complied and excelled. They have known that without English they could not have become successful. They could not have participated in their new world without the language of education and commerce. They knew that English was the language of success and that it provided them access to the common culture that holds our nation together.

Now, after all this time and generations of successful assimilation, we are being told that what has worked for so many no longer works for the current wave of immigrants. We are told that to be successful, immigrants now have to hold on to their old ways, old traditions, and most importantly their old language. They say that children suddenly need bilingual education and they say that without it, today's immigrants can't succeed. This is nonsense. Bilingual education didn't exist for decades and yet our grandparents' generations found their place in this society.

For the most part, the people clamoring for these special favors are ivory tower academics and militant Hispanics who claim it is their right to retain their language and culture, even if it is at the expense of becoming fully part of American society. Those who advocate English-only are accused of being anti-immigrant and even racist for continuing to ask our newest arrivals to learn English and to assimilate as their predecessors have done so successfully. It is said that that because we advocate for English we do not respect their rights, and want to ignore the "diversity" that immigrants bring to this country.

The real racism is in thinking that the current wave of immigrants is incapable of accomplishing what every generation before them did—assimilate and become successful. As Linda Chavez (2003) has written

> [E]ncouraging immigrants to learn English, isn't anti-Hispanic or anti-immigrant. The only reason the United States has successfully integrated so many millions of immigrants over the last 150 years is precisely because we have a common language and culture. Poles, Greeks, Italians, Jews and others learned English and came to think of themselves as Americans, which allowed them to quickly move into the cultural and economic mainstream.
>
> The key to success for today's Hispanic immigrants is to follow the same path. Ironically, the biggest impediment to this natural process is government policy, which promotes Spanish-language instead of English instruction for Hispanic children and Spanish-language services for adults.

The people who advocate bilingual education are promoting a kind of "nation within a nation" where one group is cut off from full opportunity under the false guise of "cultural pride." To promote bilingualism over the acquisition of English is divisive—it sets people apart and destroys unity.

What President Theodore Roosevelt said so well decades ago is still true today.

> There is no room in this country for hyphenated Americans. . . . The one absolutely certain way of bringing this nation to ruin, of preventing all possibility of its continuing to be a nation at all, would be to permit it to become a tangle of squabbling nationalities. We have but one flag. We must also learn one language and that language is English. (U.S. English, 2004)

Part of becoming a good citizen is taking on the values and customs of the new country and doing your best to assimilate as quickly as possible. A common language allows everyone to communicate equally and helps to foster a common set of values. To learn English is to accept those values and demonstrate a respect for the opportunities being provided by this new land. It is this common culture that sets our nation apart from others. It may be necessary for immigrants to give up a little, but what they receive in return is far more valuable.

Those who profess to support immigrants and fight for their rights to maintain their language are actually the ones doing them the greatest harm. A bunch of misguided educators would consign a whole generation of children to stay within the barriers of their own ethnic communities and keep them from branching out into the American mainstream. They would like nothing better than to encourage immigrants to stay behind the closed doors of their old ways, customs, and language.

There is one road to success in this country and that road is English. Life without English in the United States is a life without opportunity. If nothing else, it should be obvious that knowing English makes a difference in terms of dollars and cents. With a good command of English, you can earn more money than if you can't speak it well. Without a strong command of the English language, immigrants and their children are doomed to substandard, low-wage, and dead-end jobs.

The real advocates for immigrants and minorities are those of us who recognize that English is their ticket to success. Obviously, English is the language of world commerce and international dealings. Everywhere around the globe, parents clamor for their children to learn English because they know English is a key to a better life and more access to what the world has to offer. Does it make sense that the one place that people don't recognize the value of English is right here in the United States?

The Bilingual Education proponents will tell you that they do want students to learn English, just so long as it isn't at the expense of the first language. But in reality they continue to support a failed experiment. Bilingual education was originally promoted as a way to help students to bridge the gap between their first language and English. Although misguided, many no doubt were well-intentioned, thinking they were going to help students with the challenges they have always faced.

In reality this "experiment" has gone wrong and turned into something much different. Now, instead of being a quick road to success, bilingual education has become a long arduous pathway through Spanish-only for years before immigrant children are given an opportunity to learn English. What we find today are all-Spanish language programs designed to promote separatism, cultural isolationism, to promote other languages at the expense of English.

In many schools, children are prevented from even being exposed to English until late in elementary school under the false claim that it takes many years to learn a language. Some claim that it takes as long as 5 to 7 years to learn English. This is outrageous. If they are given an opportunity, children can learn English very quickly. Anyone who could think it takes that long to learn to speak English must have extremely negative beliefs about the capabilities of immigrants.

We are the ones who believe in the inherent intelligence of immigrants. We see children as young as four and five picking up English on a daily basis. But when students are forced to learn first in their native language, years are lost when students are the most adept at learning language. Research shows no benefits to delaying the introduction of English. It is only logical that to learn English you have to be exposed to it, be immersed in it, and practice it. To do otherwise is to deny common sense.

In reality the only group asking for bilingual education are Spanish speakers. All the other language groups are doing just fine without bilingual education. We have to ask why this might be. It seems that all the other groups understand that it is too confusing to learn in two languages simultaneously. They know that if they put all their effort into learning English rather than wasting their time trying to keep their first language, they learn English faster and better. Immersion is the best way to learn a language.

In addition it is just too costly to implement bilingual programs. You need extra teachers, extra classrooms, and extra materials. And these extra materials, have to be imported, making them twice as expensive. What are all the highly qualified teachers who speak English supposed to do? Bilingual programs leave them out and deprive them of their natural role in schools. At the same time, there aren't enough qualified bilingual teachers in this country. Some districts even go so far as to recruit and hire teachers from foreign countries to teach in Spanish even if they can't speak English themselves. How are they supposed to help our children learn English and succeed in school? What message does this send our students?

Another danger of bilingual programs is that they segregate students when they should be learning to work together. Instruction in these programs is focused on cultural differences instead of academics and relegates students to substandard curriculum and second class instruction. This continued separation and emphasis on other languages and cultures will only serve to factionalize our country. The common culture that holds us together will crack apart and the nation will be weakened as people retreat into separate linguistic and cultural enclaves.

Why would anyone want to deny immigrants the opportunity to participate in the richness that is the American life? Could there be some benefit to them? Could the continuing clamor by a small vocal minority be simply a case of saving their own jobs and livelihoods? It seems obvious that the only people who support Bilingual Education are the professors and the teachers whose salaries depend on a continuation of these destructive policies.

There are other negative consequences to promoting other languages over English. Instead of asking immigrants to learn English, we ask that Americans accommodate by offering translations and hiring so-called bilingual personnel. Schools give preference to people who speak another language even when their English skills are substandard. This marginalizes those who aren't bilingual from getting jobs at schools. Across the country extremely competent English speaking personnel in all kinds of positions from custodial staff to secretaries and even teachers have been replaced with far less qualified people who are hired just because they can speak some Spanish.

Bilingual education advocates demand that everything from school forms to court documents and even voting ballots be translated to accommodate those few who refuse to learn the language. This is a luxury we cannot and should not have to afford. There are over 200 languages spoken in the United States. Having government sponsored bilingual ballots and translation everywhere only removes the incentive to learn the language.

In fact, bilingual education has become a whole industry unto itself. There are bilingual outreach workers, secretaries, bilingual social workers, you name it. And these are only for the Spanish speakers. What about the children from all the other languages in our schools?

It is not that immigrants can't and shouldn't maintain their language and customs in their own homes. They can do so if they wish, but it's not the job of the schools. The best argument against bilingual education is that the very people it was supposedly designed to benefit have turned against it. Immigrant parents themselves realize that English is of great benefit and they don't want their children's time wasted in school learning a language that won't get them ahead in this country. Polls show that English is their top priority and that if they want their children to maintain their language and culture they can and should do that at home.

Everywhere you look, students who are fortunate enough to go to schools where bilingual education has been dropped to be replaced by instruction only in English are showing tremendous progress with test scores rising rapidly. That should be enough proof that English-only is the best way to go.

Comments and Questions

"English is the Glue" and You

General Questions

- Did this public argument capture your understanding of the debate over how best to address linguistic diversity in schools?
- What aspects of the argument did you agree with?
- What aspects of the argument did you disagree with?

Specific Questions

- English-only advocates propose that focusing on learning English should be the number one priority of schools. Does this English-only position adequately address all the issues raised in the cases?
- How do you respond to the proposition that to maintain a language other than English is divisive to the nation?
- Is it by definition racist and anti-immigrant to advocate for English-only instruction in school? Why or why not?

In the next few paragraphs we return to the case studies and utilize the *English is the Glue* point of view to interpret and evaluate what happened in each one. As you read, think about whether we have captured how people who share this view would analyze the cases. Does this view make more or less sense once applied to each of the cases? Do you still feel the same about this view?

The Cycle: Frank and Vu.   Frank may be worrying too much about one student's feelings. Being an immigrant is not easy and it's only logical that Vu might be feeling a little overwhelmed. The faster he learns English, the better he will feel. As long as he is getting English all the time, it shouldn't matter that much what setting it is occurring in. If he needs more ESL time, then maybe he should have it. In the meantime, Frank should keep up his high expectations and continue to do the best that he can. Perhaps Frank can look into ways that Vu can work on his English at home, as well. He and the ESL teacher could encourage his parents to use as much English as possible.

Frank might be able to make Vu more comfortable in the classroom by enlisting the help of all the students to help Vu. He could talk to the other students about how important it is for immigrant students to learn English and show them some ways they might be able to assist Vu.

Marisa's Prospects.   Marisa's problem is that she is spending entirely too much time in Spanish at home. It's great to be able to lead the neighborhood soccer game in Spanish, but that is not going to help her get a high school diploma. If she would spend the time she is wasting on translating actually studying English, she would be much farther along.

The sad thing is that she probably spent a great deal of time in elementary school in a bilingual program where she should have been learning the English she doesn't seem to have yet. Now she has to play catch up. Marisa should spend as much time as she can speaking English at home as much as possible. Maybe the school could offer English classes at night to the parents of students like Marisa so they could help their children more in English at home. It doesn't sound like this is a problem that Jane has caused. She should certainly encourage Marisa and other students like her and their families to work harder on their English.

Friendship, Professionalism, and Programs.   From the *English is the Glue* point of view, the issue is not whether Laura and Juana should be team teaching. That may or may not be helpful. The obvious reason why students aren't succeeding in the bilingual classrooms is precisely because they are not being taught enough English. They should drop these classes and focus on developing English. Because all the teachers speak English they can all teach English, so there shouldn't be any problem in dividing the Spanish speaking students more evenly among them.

The school also needs to help parents of students currently in the bilingual program understand that they are harming their children by holding them back from learning English as quickly as possible. The more that Randall can do to assimilate the new population into the American way of life the better it will be for these children and their families. They need to send a unified message that to succeed all the students must learn English quickly.

What is Equal Treatment?   It is important that immigrant students get the message that their teachers believe in them and expect they can do just as well as native English speakers. Andrew should spend his time making sure that the standards are high and don't get watered down by making baby steps for second language learners. Can't he see that the school is already losing parents who feel that the curriculum isn't challenging enough for their children?

The benchmarks should remain the same for all students. There should be a single definition of what it means to be proficient no matter where you start. It doesn't matter if they are "making progress" whatever that means. If students still can't measure up to the expectations at their grade, they will not succeed at the next level. Finally, there is no way that time should be wasted on testing students in languages other than English. This would be an irresponsible waste of resources. What matters is how much English they know and how much English they learn.

BILINGUAL EDUCATION IS A MUST

It has long been recognized that immigrants who come to America bring with them gifts and valuable resources that strengthen our nation. We are who we are as a nation today because of all we have gained by incorporating new ideas from the many cultures, perspectives, and world views that have come to our shores. But there are those who dismiss these gifts and ignore these resources all under the guise that to speak English and only English is the sign of being a good American.

There can be no argument that to become proficient in English is a critical component of success in the United States. Does this have to mean that a person can't also speak another language? The view that English alone is the path to success and prosperity is short sighted and misguided. We must consider what is lost when immigrants are told to abandon their native language and culture in order to be good citizens. The question is not whether to learn English. To be bilingual means being proficient in two languages and in the United States one of those languages, of course, must be English. To be proficient in an additional language is an advantage, strengthening and enriching a person's ability to succeed both at home and in a world economy. Supporters of bilingual education want to ensure that immigrant students not only learn English as quickly as possible, but that their academic experience be of high quality. They also want students to be allowed to benefit from the gift of bilingualism to develop their potential in life to its fullest extent. Without a doubt, the best way to promote these advantages not only to immigrant students, but to all students, would be to provide bilingual education for as many students as possible.

Bilingualism is a natural human phenomenon. Around the world people often speak more than two languages as a matter of course. Children use and learn in two or more languages on a regular basis. For most of the world, to be bilingual is the mark of a well-educated person and the advantages of speaking more than one language are valued throughout society. Bilingual education, an essential component in producing a bilingual and bi-literate society, is not limited to the United States.

Research across the globe demonstrates that children thrive and succeed in bilingual education programs. In countries with such varied immigrant populations as South Africa, Sweden, Israel, and Germany research has demonstrated that students who continue to receive support and instruction in their first language do as well as, or better, in their second language as students who receive instruction only in their second language. These same results hold true in the United States where controlled research studies consistently demonstrate that students in well-organized bilingual programs do as well or better academically in English than do their peers educated in all-English programs. The English-only advocates choose to ignore these studies and continue to spread misinformation based on false perceptions.

The debate over the best way to help immigrant children learn English has intensified over the past several decades as the number of children entering U.S. schools who speak a language other than English at home has risen dramatically. Concerns about high drop-out rates, and the low achievement of language minority students has everyone searching for explanations and cures. The "English is the Glue" proponents have erroneously placed the blame for these educational failures on bilingual education. They keep insisting that immigrant students are, in their words, "languishing in bilingual classes." It would be wonderful if most immigrant students were receiving bilingual education, but they are not. The truth is that the vast majority of these students (90%) don't receive any kind of primary language support, much less a fully implemented bilingual education program. If second language learners as a group are failing, then they are being failed by the all-English programs most of them already attend. If the English-only people were truly concerned about the academic achievement of immigrant students, they would be examining the kind and quality of instruction that immigrant students receive in English.

Opponents of bilingual education act as if all-English programs would automatically guarantee success. If English alone were the pathway to success then how do they explain that the greatest crisis in American schools today is not with new immigrants? The groups who are least well served in this country and who are failing at disproportionate rates are African-American students and second- and third-generation students from immigrant families who speak only English. The problem with the "give them English and they will succeed" argument is that it confounds the problems of language with that of race and class. The educational system routinely overlooks the needs of poor and minority students, no matter what language background they come from. These students are relegated to substandard schools, with less qualified teachers and subjected to a curriculum that has little relevance to their lives or history.

Educational success depends on much more than speaking or not speaking English. It depends on providing high quality instruction to all. Nonetheless, although learning English is no guarantee, given the context of racism and oppression of people of color, proficiency in English is a critical element to being successful and productive in the United States. Immigrant students do need to, and have the right to be able to speak, read, and write English well.

Linguists, language acquisition specialists, and civil rights activists all agree that bilingual education is a fundamentally sound educational alternative that helps students learn English as quickly as possible. Why does bilingual education work? It's simple. It allows students to continue to learn and apply important concepts and knowledge in their first language at the same time that they are learning English. It should be evident to everyone that it is easier to learn new ideas and especially how to read in a language you understand. Then, what you know in one language, you can learn to express in the other as you gain fluency.

Think of what it takes to learn to read. You have to figure out that abstract squiggles on paper represent sounds you can say, and that when you put them together they represent words you know. This is hard enough in your first language. What happens when you can "sound it out" but don't know the meaning of the word that the sounds represent? Millions of second language learners have become good at sounding out, but that hasn't made them good readers. It makes much more sense for children to learn to read in their home language, a language already understood, and then transfer those understandings to English.

It is hard to imagine why anyone would want to make the path to learning more difficult for any child, and why so many people in this country are afraid of bilingual education. Could it be because most Americans are monolingual English speakers whose only exposure to another language has been through high school foreign language classes at which they failed miserably? Because the vast majority of people in the United States have not managed to become academically bilingual, let alone achieve basic communication skills in another language, they can't conceive that young children, many of them from poor and undereducated families, could possibly do so. Or, maybe the real threat is the competitive advantage that poor immigrant children would have over their own children in the job market if these students' bilingual potential were fully realized.

Many people mistakenly think that bilingual education is a recent issue that has to do mainly with coddling Spanish speaking immigrants. This is reflected in the current popular myth that bilingual education means "Spanish-only programs." They argue that all previous generations made it without all this help. To the contrary there have been bilingual education programs in what is now the United States even before it became a nation. Some of the earliest and most extensive programs were German–English programs. Their existence, however, has always hinged upon the particular political winds blowing at the moment.

The only real opposition to bilingual education comes from outside the field. The loudest outcry comes from politicians and business people who have little, or nothing to do with, or understanding of how children learn. Those who argue for English-only under the pretense of doing what is best for immigrants are at best uninformed. At worst their mean-spirited opposition to bilingual education usually has ulterior political motives. Ignoring all research that clearly demonstrates that bilingual education is as effective as all English instruction, and often more so in creating proficient English speakers, they continue to claim falsely that it doesn't work. In several states these extreme opponents of bilingual education have actually duped the public into criminalizing the teaching of content in a language other than English—even if it is the only language a child can understand. In three states, they have gone so far as to put into law that teachers can be sued if they use a child's first language in instruction. In reality those who oppose bilingual education are practicing a form of linguistic cleansing. Their agenda has nothing to do with pedagogy and everything to do with racism, xenophobia, and anti-immigrant sentiments.

The English-only movement fans the flames against bilingual education by spreading the baseless claim that today's immigrants won't learn English unless they are forced to. It is a prevailing but absolutely false perception that immigrants are no longer learning English. Though this myth persists, there is absolutely no evidence to back it up. Today's immigrants and their descendants are learning English at the same rate as previous generations. Opponents of bilingual education also overlook that many former immigrants did not, in fact, need to learn English well to guarantee their success to the extent that it takes today to succeed in our society. Many were able to succeed where physical labor was a primary source of employment. Now, in an information society, English language learning at that most basic level can no longer guarantee success.

Far from being in danger, English continues to be the language of power, of commerce and of popular culture. Analysis of census data and surveys of immigrants themselves show clearly that by the second generation most immigrants including Spanish speakers, have abandoned their first language and have joined the ranks of monolingual English speakers.

Educators and the larger society have both a moral and a legal obligation to support the best educational practices for immigrant students and language minority children. A decent education is a fundamental cornerstone to the guarantee of life, liberty, and the pursuit of happiness outlined in our constitution. The promise of an education for all is one of things that sets our nation apart from others and makes it such an attractive destination for those seeking a better life.

There is a long standing and firm legal basis for providing students instruction in their native language while they are learning English. For example, at the end of the Mexican American War the people living in the land that was taken from Mexico in 1848—now the states of California, Arizona, New Mexico, Texas, and part of Colorado—had their citizenship changed from Mexican to United States overnight. However, the Treaty of Guadalupe Hidalgo was supposed to have guaranteed them continued access to their language and culture.

More recently, in the case of *Lau v. Nichols*, the U.S. Supreme Court recognized and affirmed that under civil rights law districts needed to take "affirmative steps" to help students overcome language barriers if second language learners of English were to have equal access to the curriculum (Crawford, 2000). It may surprise current day opponents of bilingual education that this case, which resulted in such a far-reaching decision, was brought 30 years ago by the parents of Chinese immigrant students and not Spanish speakers in California.

Several conditions existed in California at that time. School was mandatory for children between the ages of 6 and 16, English was the official language of instruction and in order to graduate from high school students had to prove they knew English. The plaintiffs in the Lau case argued that the school district was not providing an appropriate education to the non-English-speaking Chinese students, an education that would give them access to learning and allow them to graduate. They further argued that simply providing the same curriculum in English to the Chinese speaking students did not provide equal educational opportunity. This, they reasoned, meant that the educational rights of the students under the Equal Protection Clause of the Fourteenth Amendment were being violated. The Supreme Court agreed.

In August 1974, the Equal Educational Opportunities Act affirmed the Lau decision and expanded its jurisdiction "to apply to all public school districts, not just those receiving federal financial assistance." The act requires educational agencies to "take appropriate action to overcome language barriers that impede equal participation by students in their instructional programs." These cases and many others filed in state and federal courts across the country, should legally bind public schools wherever possible to provide to students instruction in a language they can understand (McPherson, 2000).

Even if it weren't mandated, bilingual education should still be available because it provides the only real opportunity in this country for children to become academically bilingual. Bilingualism is of social and intellectual value to the individual, it helps to strengthen communities, and it provides a significant advantage in the global economy that helps bolster our nation's competitiveness in the world.

To be bilingual is more than just knowing two different languages. The presence of the two languages in the speakers' brains provides them with increased cognitive flexibility. Bilinguals have access to ways of understanding language and can manipulate language to express their ideas in ways that cannot be achieved through only one language. This is known as metalinguistic awareness—the ability to think abstractly about language. The resulting heightened cognitive development translates into stronger academics. It doesn't matter which two languages, just being bilingual is better.

Another advantage of being bilingual is the ability to communicate with people from more than one linguistic background and thereby from different cultural backgrounds. This can serve to provide more harmonious intercultural relations and increase opportunities for people from differing perspectives to communicate and jointly solve problems. These are skills sorely needed in today's increasingly global economy given the increasing tensions and misunderstandings among the world's peoples.

Some of the strongest proponents of bilingual education are monolingual English speaking teachers in all English programs who are actually begging for primary language support to be provided to their students. They know it will help the students learn and that it will provide them and other teachers the ability to truly communicate with the students and their families.

Encouraging families to maintain and utilize their home language with their children makes for stronger family relationships and increases the likelihood that students will stay in school. It is not just that people have a right to their language and culture. When schools seek to eliminate languages other than English, students very often lose the ability to talk to relatives and community members, which compounds the disintegration of many immigrant families. Some attribute high gang rates among immigrant students to this breakdown in the ability to communicate with their families. As they become estranged from their home language and culture, they seek out gangs for a sense of belonging.

By valuing students' home language, schools can actually enhance academic performance in English. Misguided attempts to impose English-only mandates, harm not only immigrant children, but limit the opportunities for native English speaking students to participate in bilingual education programs, as well. The best bilingual education programs are those that maintain the use of the first language in instruction over time, instead of just using it as a small stepping stone to learning English. Among the most successful programs are those that also involve native English speakers in becoming bilingual. Efforts to eliminate bilingual education take away all parents' right to choose such a program for their children.

Comments and Questions

"Bilingual Education is a Must" and You

General Questions

- Did this public argument capture your understanding of the debate over how best to address linguistic diversity in schools?
- What aspects of the argument did you agree with?
- What aspects of the argument did you disagree with?

Specific Questions

- Do advocates of bilingual education adequately address the need of immigrants to learn English? Are they overlooking anything?
- Is this position realistic given the numbers of languages and cultures represented in public schools today?
- What would your prospects for employment be in a school where the development of bilingualism for students is a top priority? Would you need to do anything differently from what you are currently doing? Why or why not?

The Cycle: Frank and Vu.   A lot of Vu's problems would be solved if he were given more opportunity to learn through his native language. Instead of asking whether Vu should be getting more or less ESL, Frank should be trying to figure out how he could get him some support in his first language. He should see if the school could provide a primary language tutor for Vu either to teach him to read in his first language or at least to help him with the big ideas of the subject matter he is learning.

Obviously Vu is capable or he wouldn't be so frustrated by his slow progress. Part of the reason Vu might be acting out is because he can sense that he is seen as a problem for the teacher. Or he might feel like he doesn't belong in the classroom. Frank could do a lot more to help all the students in the class value Vu's language and culture. He could ask Vu and his family to teach a lesson to the class. He could help them see how challenging it is to learn a second language by having them try to learn something in Vu's language. Frank could put up pictures of Vu's home country and have books in his home language available for Vu to take home to read with his parents. The sooner Frank starts acting on the belief that Vu's first language is a vehicle for learning, the faster his relationship with Vu will improve.

Marisa's Prospects.   Jane should be commended for taking the time and the trouble to go to Marisa's home and meet her family. It is unfortunate that she was so surprised by what she found. The fact that Marisa's parents are very supportive is typical of most Spanish-speaking parents despite the stereotypes. It is crucial that Jane go ahead and act on the new understandings she has gained.

First and foremost, Jane needs to find a way to build on Marisa's academic skills in Spanish. She needs someone to help Marisa transfer the skills she has in Spanish to her work in English without translating. For example, Jane could also try finding materials in Spanish that Marisa could use at home without having to translate.

Another thing that could help would be to help organize some community outreach. Maybe Jane and her colleagues could organize a class for parents in how best to help secondary students with their homework. They could give them examples in Spanish of the kinds of questions and discussions in that are likely to be the most beneficial. Jane should also take her findings to the school district and request that there be a process established for teachers across schools to systematically share information about second language learners who move from level to level. Although it may take effort on her part, if Jane can change how the other teachers view students like Marisa, the work of all of them will be made easier and many students and teachers will benefit.

Friendship, Professionalism, and Programs.   It is an excellent idea for Laura and Juana to team teach to build on the strengths of both teachers. This will open new opportunities for many students. Laura and her colleagues will find that their concerns about the bilingual program are unfounded. At the same time the students in those classes are learning English, they also will be learning how to read and do content area work in Spanish. In this way their academic development won't be held back.

As for Laura's concern about how her English-speaking colleagues will respond to her, there may be some difficult moments. The time has probably come for the teachers at the school to face up to the reality that it is an advantage to be bilingual. Given the increasing population of second language learners at schools like Randall, teachers with two languages should be given priority over monolingual teachers in any new hiring that occurs following the retreat until the staff is balanced with regard to its needs. But as long as the monolingual English speaking teachers are willing to work collaboratively as Laura has offered to do, there should always be place for them in the school.

What is Equal Treatment?   Andrew is right to be concerned about the misuse of tests designed for native English speakers. They will never provide accurate information about what second language learners actually know. Wherever possible, students should be able to demonstrate their understandings of content area instruction in their first language. This may not be possible for all languages, but that shouldn't prevent the school from using assessments in languages other than English where they exist. Otherwise every test is really a test of English and not of the students' knowledge of the content area.

Where students can't be tested in their first language they should be able to take versions of tests that have been adapted specifically for second language learners. These tests would need to be designed to take into account that students are learning both English and content and not penalize them if they know the content, but make errors with language. The kinds of benchmarks and indicators that Andrew is advocating are essential in developing this kind of assessment. They should be developed and made available to every teacher in the district. Finally, not only should Andrew push forward with his idea of creating benchmarks in English for second language learners, he should also insist that benchmarks be developed in any other languages in which students are being taught in bilingual programs.

A PRAGMATIC APPROACH

As the previous arguments indicate, the constant flow of new immigrants to the United States brings with it both tremendous opportunities and constant challenges for our nation. The debate never seems to end over how to best integrate newcomers into the fabric of American society. Many say that public education has been the key factor in guaranteeing that previous generations of immigrants have succeeded. Others claim that lack of equal access to education has actually prevented many immigrants from fully engaging in the economic prosperity that this country offers.

With every new wave of immigrants seeking a better life, the volatile issues of assimilation and acculturation resurface, embodied primarily in arguments over the need to learn English. Disagreements about how best to educate immigrant students reflect polarized positions fully entrenched in political ideology as embodied by both the "English is the Glue" and "Bilingual Education is a Must" points of view.

By definition people coming from other nations represent differing viewpoints, ways of life, priorities, and languages. In addition, many immigrants are people of color who are often poor. It is hardly surprising, then, that their presence pushes many political buttons.

As schools become more culturally and linguistically diverse teachers find themselves caught between competing ideologies. Too often, programs are designed based on which configuration will take the least political heat, even in the face of evidence that might support a different structure and approach for successfully educating second language learners. Although the multiplicity of political opinions must be recognized, the choices that individual schools, districts and states make about what kinds of programs to offer students should be based on what is pedagogically most effective. And for the most part, effectiveness depends on the quality of instruction.

Unfortunately, neither the passion of the "English-only" camp for producing "good" Americans nor the passion of the "Bilingual Education is a Must" camp for producing global citizens is sufficient to address the complexity of the challenges facing today's schools. Bilingualism is a good thing and the benefits to students who receive instruction in their primary language instruction as they learn English are many. However, to provide a bilingual program for all students who could benefit from one is not usually feasible. It is not racist to say that all-English programs can work, nor is it nation dividing to advocate for the benefits of a bilingual education.

There are no easy solutions or quick fixes for the challenges that linguistic diversity poses. Daily, students arrive in schools at every grade level from many languages and cultures, a variety of experiences, and differing academic backgrounds. The responsibility of educators is to maximize the academic achievement of every child who arrives at school, whatever it takes. Arguments about how to run schools that are based in political ideology alone do little to help teachers in their interactions with students and their families.

One of the challenges facing educators is a mindset common in the society at large and prevalent in many schools, that sees students who do not speak English as somehow broken. Within this paradigm, the teachers' job is to "repair" them. This can result in a climate where professionals are pitted against each other in a finger pointing blame game of whose job it is to "fix" the students.

The students, however, are by no means broken. They simply don't speak English. What they need is for teachers to wisely and effectively provide them with the best instruction possible using all of the particular resources of their school setting. They also need strong school leadership and a commitment to the shared responsibility by everyone in the school.

To accommodate the broad variation among the needs of students, the entire system must be challenged to provide appropriate instruction. Educators need to organize themselves so that throughout the entire day every teacher's instruction provides students the time, experiences and opportunities they need to fully develop academic proficiency. Any school-wide process or plan in a linguistically diverse setting should address the nature and quality of instruction, establishing benchmarks for students' progress through programs, ways to reach out to, and involve, parents, families and community members and planning for cross-cultural interactions.

Many teachers and administrators fear that second language students are going to end up being "terminal second language learners." They want to know why even after 2–4 years of special programming, many second language learners are still not classified as fluent English speakers. The English-only camp explains everything by saying it is because of the harmful effects of using students' native language instruction, although less than a third of these students in this country actually receive this type of instruction. Those at the other end of the spectrum, who argue for primary language instruction for all children, say it is a racist system that denies students' the use of their native language and devalues their cultures that is to blame.

It is not simply the presence or absence of a child's first language in instruction that accounts for academic achievement. Students' success or failure has everything to do with the nature and quality of the instruction they receive throughout their school day, no matter what language it is in. Too often, educators focus on finding the one right program or the best model for instructional delivery. Instead of focusing on which program model is best, it is more important to become familiar with the broader concepts of organization for academic and linguistic success. For example, in every kind of program, including all English programs, the first language plays an important role whether or not it is used directly in school instruction and needs to be valued as a tool for learning. In addition, it is also essential that every program must include direct instruction in English for at least part of every day. Because the way each language is used impacts the other, the differing ways to organize instruction that result from these language use decisions all require careful planning. The less access to primary language the more English instruction will need to be modified to make concepts understandable and to develop full linguistic proficiency simultaneously in all areas of the curriculum.

To understand students' progress in their second language, it is vital to determine what kind of instruction they have received. For example, when considering a student's progress, the following questions are important:

- Was it 2 years of pull-out ESL for 30–45 minutes 3 times a week?
- Or, was it a comprehensive coordinated program where all teachers who worked with the children were purposefully differentiating their instruction to make it comprehensible to all students?

- Was there any primary language instruction?
- If so, was it used for conceptual reinforcement or merely to discipline students?
- Were students always integrated with native English speakers and never given time to work specifically on communication and the structures and forms of the language itself?
- Conversely, were students put into a completely segregated instructional space, where despite hearing English in their instruction, they never had an opportunity to interact or communicate with native speakers?
- What criteria were used to reclassify students as "Fluent English proficient"—minimal oral criteria or a thorough assessment of their performance in reading, writing, and the content areas?
- Do teachers understand that some of their students who are currently labeled as "fluent English speakers" were just months before classified as having limited proficiency in English?
- Do they understand the development of higher levels of proficiency in English and students' ongoing need for support?

Each school is unique in the population it serves, the preparation of its staff, and the resources it has available. Therefore, it may need to be unique in the ways that it incorporates understandings of what is commonly referred to as "best practice." These best practices should be used to create a district framework that supports individual school planning. Bilingual education supporters who argue that without primary language instruction students can't learn English may well take exception to the idea that there can be excellent all-English programs. Proponents of all English instruction will reject any program that includes the use of the primary language regardless of its excellence and the benefits it can accrue to the students. These entrenched positions are counterproductive and overlook reality.

What Does It Take to Create Proficient English Speakers?   Even under optimal circumstances it takes several years to become fully academically proficient in a second language. It is a developmental process that requires a student's growth to be monitored. If students have been educated in their home countries, the process moves more quickly because those students have background academic knowledge (e.g., they already know how to read and write in one language and, therefore, have academic tools to transfer to English). Estimates of the length of time it takes to become fully academically proficient generally range from 4 to 7 years or longer for students who arrive without academic preparation in their first language (Collier, 1989, 1992; Cummins, 2000). No amount of wishing can change that.

The particular school students attend will greatly affect their academic achievement and life opportunities. Many systemic pressures work against the academic success of language minority students. But it is clearly evident that some schools do a far better job than others in working with them. How are some schools better able to equip immigrant students with the kinds of skills they need to succeed in the United States? How do they manage and utilize the complex interactions of language, culture, and context that surround linguistic diversity to help students succeed? The answers to these questions lie in the nature of the instruction provided to students and the attitudes of the adults who work with them daily in schools. With that in mind, let us look at the arguments of both camps.

Problems With the English-Only Point of View

Given the vehemence of the opposition to bilingual education, one would imagine it was the predominant program type for second language learners. Actually, it is the exception in the United States. Despite the rhetoric of the English-only camp, the great majority of second language learners of English already receive all of their instruction in English. Even before the passage of the antibilingual education propositions in California, Arizona, and Massachusetts more than two out of three of the students learning English as a second language were in all English programs (Macias, 1997, 1998; Mora, 2003). In addition, many programs defined as "bilingual" are called that because the children who attend them don't speak English, but they provide minimal, if any, support in the first language. If the majority of second language learners in the country aren't performing as desired, then all-English instruction bears much of the responsibility for the lack of student progress that has been documented nationwide.

The English-only people will tell you that it is only logical that the fastest route to English proficiency is through all English instruction. They add that it's too complicated to teach in more than one language and it simplifies everything if everyone is teaching in just one language. Many assume that simply being in English all day should suffice. Overlooking the fact that second language learners have special needs, teachers in programs based on this assumption teach as if all students were native English speakers. Even where second language students' need for modified instruction is recognized, these students are too often relegated to a certain set of teachers who deliver instruction through a curriculum that is considered somehow different from, and substandard to, the "real" curriculum.

At the heart of the English-only position is the major misperception that what students learn in a language other than English takes away from their learning of English. In this view, primary language instruction is just a waste of time and resources. The truly ignorant go so far as to say that if you don't know something in English, then you don't really know anything at all. Knowledge in the primary language is not valued, either with regard to what students arrive with or what they might add in their first language as they grow and develop. This is a mistake.

Ironically, one of the most important reasons to use the primary language where possible is precisely that it shortens the time needed to acquire academic proficiency in English. Yes, it is counterintuitive. It only seems logical that "the more English the better." But students have far more than the English language to learn. They must also learn the curriculum content, the same task facing native English speakers.

Students who are taught in a language they don't know are more likely to miss out on most of the instruction. Therefore, the less access students have to learning in their first language, the longer it will take to become fully academically proficient in English. Using the primary language provides direct access to the content. This supports students in continuing to learn content as they become more and more proficient in English and can then learn more and more through English.

If this is still confusing, then imagine you have moved to China where, after 2 years of preparation you and your family will live for many years. You have barely learned any Chinese, but you place your children in Chinese schools and enroll in a Chinese language program yourself. After 5 months, you have been asked to make a presentation in Chinese to your high school-aged child's classmates about the three major religious traditions in the United States. You are well versed in your own religion, but unfortunately know little about any others. Learning about the other religions and learning to talk about them in Chinese at the same time will likely seem overwhelming. If you were only able to learn about the unfamiliar religions through Chinese, it would probably slow you down quite a bit. It is certainly logical that you will want to and will benefit from using English, your primary language, to learn as much about other religious traditions as quickly as possible. At the same time, you can continue to learn and practice the structure of the Chinese. Then you can begin to express what you have learned about the topic using the language you are acquiring. If your language instruction is centered around the ideas and vocabulary of the religious traditions you are studying, rather than shopping or clothing, you will likely be able to put the two parts together more quickly.

Just Using English Is Not Enough.   Too often, those who admonish educators to "just use English" seem to imply that it's the easy solution, requiring little additional thought or planning. Of course, it is possible to learn new ideas, new concepts, and even to read in a second language, but success is dependent on the kinds of strategies that teachers use. If, for example, you are reading a text and don't know what "flat bottomed boat" means, you have the task not only of decoding the words, but of understanding what is being communicated through the text. If students are going to be able to learn well in a language they don't speak, teachers will have to significantly modify how they teach to them. It takes a good deal of knowledge, extra planning, and additional work to make instruction understandable and effective.

Unfortunately many teachers don't see this as their job. They see it as the job of the ESL teacher to teach English and their job to teach their content, without regard to using methods and strategies that will make it more understandable for second language learners. Although students will spend the majority of their time in the regular classroom (80–90%), many teachers still do not see the need to improve the quality of instruction during this time. So, in most all-English settings (and in the English portion of some bilingual programs), teachers keep using strategies best suited for native English speakers. This leaves second language learners to "get the content" on their own (or not). Place yourself back in your Chinese classroom with all native Chinese speakers. What challenges would you encounter?

With appropriate instruction, it is possible for students to learn English without access to their primary language in instruction. The question arises, however, whether simply learning English is a sufficient outcome of schooling given that there are greater benefits that can be reaped beyond English proficiency alone. One result of all-English instruction is that most students who attend these programs end up being monolingual English speakers. In a process known as subtractive bilingualism, they lose their first language and replace it with English. This is problematic for a variety of reasons. One very troubling aspect is that if English instruction has not been of high quality, as students lose their first language, they may only attain minimal academic competency in English language leaving them with weakened access to their funds of knowledge in either language. As their first language is lost, students may also lose their connections with their families. This, in turn, will limit their family's ability to be involved with and influential in the lives of their children (Wong Fillmore, 1989).

In addition to the possibility of a subtractive academic experience and alienation from the fundamental family unit, students with the potential to achieve full bilingual proficiency are denied that opportunity. These students will never reap the benefits that accrue to people who are bilingual. That lost resource affects the individual, the community, and the nation. And it is an unnecessary loss. The fact is we can do more in schools than turn out only monolingual English speakers. We can produce bilingual students capable of doing academic work in more than one language, making it an additive experience for second language learners and native speakers of English students, as well.

Problems With the "Bilingual Education Is a Must" Point of View

It is possible to share many of the understandings and views put forward by those who feel that bilingual education is a must and still not advocate a 'bilingual education at any cost' mindset. The main concern is that strict adherence to the demand for primary language instruction without attention paid to quality of instruction can result in weak and ineffective programs. As with any kind of program, truly successful bilingual programs adhere to certain quality standards that guide the development of successful instruction in two languages.

All-English Settings. Viewpoints regarding the need and ability to use the students' primary language are shaped by and positions are taken in response to local conditions and prior experiences. Many vocal advocates of bilingual education work in communities where there is just one major immigrant group and native language resources are readily available. They may fail to understand the challenges of a school where there are multiple languages represented and few, if any, resources (human or material) to teach well in any or most of them. Teaching all in English may be the only viable option. This will take careful planning, knowledge of second language instructional methods, and an understanding of assessment and benchmarks for successful achievement. And this doesn't mean that one must advocate that English is the only important language.

There are many ways to value bilingualism and the primary language in a school where instruction is all in English. Successful all-English programs encourage families to continue to nurture the primary language outside of school. They encourage parents to stay fully involved with their children using the language in which parents feel most comfortable and proficient. Such schools also provide an environment that reflects a respect for other languages and cultures. For example, these schools post welcome signs in many languages. And, they maintain multilingual library collections that are available for use by students and their families. They facilitate access to community-based resources that can support primary language development outside of school. Unfortunately, because many all-English programs don't value the primary language, they usually fail to fully incorporate the students and their families into the mainstream of school life. This separates the family from a major experience in their child's life, a very negative outcome and one that is by no means inevitable.

Some proponents of bilingual education tell you that without primary language instruction, second language learners will never become academically proficient in English. In part, they don't believe that monolingual English speaking teachers are capable of effectively teaching students with whom they can't communicate. There are, however, many examples of excellent monolingual English speaking teachers who work successfully every day to help students who speak languages the teachers don't speak. These teachers do everything they can to use appropriate methods and strategies to modify their instruction to make it accessible to these students. They value these students' culture, their language, and their families, integrating them into their classroom and school. They also make sure that children are supported in moving forward in continually more sophisticated levels of learning rather than staying stuck in simplistic levels of instruction.

Failure to Plan Well for the Use of Each Language.   The way in which languages are used in programs for second language learners is a major aspect in instruction planning. In successful bilingual programs, decisions about which language to use, for what purpose, and with which students, are not left up to individual teachers. Rather, the school has a clear roadmap for the development of the languages across grade levels. As mentioned earlier, acquiring language takes time, purposeful planning and benchmarks. The balance of languages across time and the curriculum is critical for the development of full academic proficiency. In the absence of thoughtful planning the mere presence of the primary language in instruction will not guarantee success and may limit students' access to and development of academic language skills.

Failure to Expose Students to the Full Curriculum.   Another area that requires careful planning is the content and format of instruction. In strong bilingual programs there is consistency from grade level to grade level, and classroom to classroom. The curriculum in the bilingual strand does not differ significantly in topic and scope from the "real" curriculum in English. Decisions made that ignore this understanding can result in discrepancies between what is taught in different programs even within the same school. The pervasive misperception among the public that students in bilingual programs are just marking time until they get into the real program or are "mainstreamed" is sometimes fueled by real differences in curriculum, especially in social studies. Planners in some schools place an over-emphasis on topics that relate to the specific culture of the students, which can lead to the exclusion of other topics that it is assumed all students at a particular grade level will learn. When this occurs, gaps in students' knowledge base are created. This, of course, need not be the case with good planning and a balanced, culturally sensitive curriculum, but too often is.

As with all-English programs, strong bilingual programs are predicated on having well qualified personnel that can teach in both languages—in this case personally or in teams. Sometimes, however, schools will attempt to implement a bilingual program even when there aren't enough fully qualified personnel available to deliver all the parts of a good program, convinced of the need for primary language instruction, no matter what. Teachers designated as bilingual or as proficient in the target language can range from native speakers of that language who are fully academically prepared, to native English speakers who lack the fundamental fluency in the target language needed to teach at a cognitively challenging level. Some schools even hire teachers because they promise they will learn the target language over the summer or in a couple of years. This again underscores the prevailing lack of understanding regarding quality language development. Imagine having your native English-speaking child in a classroom with a native French or other language speaker who has had only 2 years of preparation in English. This would be unacceptable to most English speaking parents, yet these actions are taken in some bilingual programs in the name of valuing the primary language. As much as we support the goals, when the choice is having poor instruction in the native language or really superior to excellent instruction in English, the balance can shift. Again, the question is not whether or not there should be primary language, but how we can use the available resources to effectively promote academic success.

Summary

Political and social views, perceptions, and biases influence our view of students in schools and the ways we organize for students' instruction. Any approach to providing excellent instruction should avoid using political criteria to determine educational program. Simplistic all-or-nothing "one way or the other" solutions will not work. All kinds of programs can either be successful or disastrous depending on the decisions made about how to deliver instruction.

Working Together. Second language learners are second language learners of English all day long not just during certain periods of the day. We can no longer afford to deceive ourselves that the ESL or bilingual teachers are single-handedly responsible for a child's academic success and it can't be "us and them." All teachers must be provided with, and expected to use, strategies to differentiate instruction to meet the various needs of their students. In all-English programs, in order to make significant advances in both language development and academic skills, students need to receive instruction throughout the day from all their teachers that addresses their needs as second language learners. In programs that include primary language instruction what is taught in both languages should be coordinated across the day and full advantage taken of the time spent in each language.

It is pragmatic to seek common ground and we believe that everyone has a role in the education of language minority students. It doesn't make sense for schools to mandate that educators can't use a language other than English or on the other hand that they must. School staff need to work together to create a positive and effective environment for language learning. In all programs there are ways to organize even limited resources to optimize student achievement both in and outside of school (Miramontes et al., 1997). In planning programs for second language learners of English the question is not whether to use the student's primary language, but rather how much of the students' primary language can be used effectively in instruction.

A pragmatic approach advocates for the use of primary language when possible, while at the same time accepts that an all-English program can be successful. Both sides need to acknowledge that the use of the students' first language is beneficial if used appropriately, and at the same time recognize it is not the only option where it is not feasible. Any plan should pay attention to consistency within and across grade levels and the entire school. The issues raised with regards to bilingual education are not a basis for eliminating the use of students' primary language in instruction. Rather, they are an argument for quality control.

Comments and Questions

"A Pragmatic Approach" and You

General Questions

- Did this public argument capture your understanding of the debate over how best to address linguistic diversity in schools?
- What aspects of the argument did you agree with?
- What aspects of the argument did you disagree with?

Specific Questions

- Are pragmatists actually refusing to take a stand about what is important in the education of language minority students?
- Is it realistic to be pragmatic? Can every school really decide for itself what kind of program to offer? Why or why not?
- How prepared do you feel to take part in a decision-making process that depends on well developed understandings of language acquisition, bilingualism and cultural diversity? What kind of information would you need to participate effectively? Do you have other priorities at this point in your career? Should you?

The Cycle: Frank and Vu. The greatest concern regarding Frank's dilemma is not whether Vu needs ESL services from Betsy. The real problem in this situation is that individual teachers are left on their own to make this kind of decision. Apparently there is no articulated plan for the delivery of services to second language learners. Not only the school, but the district as a whole should have established criteria based on formal assessments for who receives services and what form these services should take.

Second language learners like Vu who are learning both the English language and the curriculum in English need instruction tailored to their needs throughout the school day. It is not a case of one or the other, whether it is Betsy or Frank who holds the responsibility for Vu's performance. Frank is not a failure because Vu needs continued ESL support. And in one hour a day, Betsy can't possibly address all of Vu's needs. The administrator in the building needs to help foster a climate of shared responsibility and create a plan for second language learners that is not subject to the whims and feelings of individual teachers.

Marisa's Prospects.   Jane would do well to summarize her findings in a memo to her principal in which she shares her enthusiasm and ask to be connected with others who are reaching out to the Spanish-speaking community. Perhaps her ideas could be put on the agenda of a faculty meeting. It is safe to assume that there are many students like Marisa at her school whose language proficiency background is overlooked and whose skills in their first language are ignored. School wide the teachers could come up with some strategies to support Marisa and others like her. They could institutionalize the idea of home visits and share the responsibility. They could organize an intensive class for students who are fluent readers and writers in Spanish to help them transfer these academic skills to English. They could identify major topics in the curriculum and accumulate resources in other languages to give to families to support them in their work with their children at home.

Friendship, Professionalism and Programs.   Laura and Juana have gotten the school moving in the right direction. They are fortunate to have an administrator who is willing to move beyond his current comfort zone and tackle this complicated issue. They may also be able to avoid the pitfalls that come with trying to make changes on their own without coordinating with what is happening in the rest of the school. The retreat itself will be very important for establishing the kind of dialogue that needs to occur so that all teachers can take part in building the strongest program possible. They will need to discuss openly and honestly how the teachers feel about the changes to their school and what it means for their roles.

As people enter the retreat they should try to leave behind their preconceived notions about what "bilingual education" looks like. They should be trying to figure out how they can make the most use of the Spanish abilities of the bilingual staff. Whatever they decide it will be important for all teachers to commit to the new structure and work to communicate within and across the grade levels. There should be school-wide staff development regarding strategies that are effective for differentiation and especially for working with second language learners. The most important goal of the retreat should be that every teacher in the school take ownership for the success of the second language learners.

What is Equal Treatment?   Andrew is moving in the right direction. It is probably time for him to invite someone to speak to the committee about demographic trends and the increase in the number of second language learners district wide. This might help the teachers who are not currently affected to see that the committee's work should address the wider population of students in the district. Andrew can be comforted knowing that the committee doesn't have to reinvent the wheel. If he did a little extra investigation he would find that a substantial amount of work has already been done in many states and at the national level to create standards and benchmarks for students learning English as their second language. They could adopt some of these or use them as models for their own Language Arts standards.

Andrew might also try to lead the committee in a brainstorming session about how the big ideas represented in the standards can be demonstrated in multiple ways. How could students demonstrate their understandings of a standard such as: "Literature from around the world constitutes a record of human experience" other than through a paper and pencil test? It may be possible then for the committee to see that work prompted by the needs of the second language learners can benefit all students, particularly those who may not yet be strong readers and writers.

III

FINAL ARGUMENTS AND SOME SUGGESTIONS AND RESOURCES FOR FURTHER REFLECTION

In this final section, we accomplish three distinct tasks. We present the main elements of our own point of view in terms of the public arguments you have just read. We offer suggestions for further reflection and we provide a bibliography of resources to assist you in your ongoing reflective process.

The underlying framework for this book series is reflective practice. It is important to ground your reflections within a clear understanding of your own and others' points of view regarding critical issues. The public arguments presented in the previous section provide three specific points of view of how best to address the challenges of linguistic diversity. Most of us will find some merit in each of the arguments and disagree with other aspects. Informed reflection allows us to better recognize the elements of a particular argument in order to sort through them and understand their various ramifications.

You can enhance the reflective process by broadening your experience base. It is valuable to inquire formally and informally into the world around you and then reflect upon it. In this way you can begin to compare and contrast what happens in different circumstances and how you respond to each situation. This can be done in many ways, both in and out of schools. To that end, we outline some activities, exercises, and questions that can extend your reflections regarding the topics covered in this book. All the ideas are intended to illuminate how schools and their personnel respond to linguistic diversity. They include observations of classrooms, interviews with community members, home visits, the analysis of instructional materials, and gaining new experiences. It is our hope that you will be encouraged to try some, inquire, and reflect further.

Finally, we present a bibliography of books and articles that can serve as resources for further reflection and provide additional information helpful in working in linguistically diverse schools. This bibliography includes both works referenced in this volume and other valuable tools to help you prepare for the challenges that undoubtedly await you. If you cannot find these resources in your college or university library, they are accessible through an interlibrary loan process.

OUR PERSPECTIVE

The four cases that comprise the first section of this book and the public arguments that follow describe issues that confront most teachers in the nation. The increasing linguistic diversity of today's public schools brings with it changes and challenges that very often are viewed negatively. We choose to view these changes in a positive light, and believe that they provide educators with unexpected and exciting opportunities. By considering linguistic diversity as a given instead of second language learners as a problem, many possibilities emerge for improving the academic achievement of all students. By rethinking our approaches to education we can reach a broader segment of the population, no matter their language background. By embracing students' differences and organizing ourselves around common understandings, we can create better schools for everyone.

External variables impact decision making in schools. The efforts to educate second language learners will interact with the volatile political context that surrounds linguistic and cultural diversity. A clear understanding of community needs, concerns, and issues and how to work together will contribute greatly to effective decision making. Rather than accepting an all-or-none position about which program or model is best, educators would benefit more by making programmatic decisions based on a deeper understanding of three areas. These are: the nature of first and second language acquisition; the relationship of students' learning in their first and second languages; and specific strategies for instruction that allow second language learners to access the curriculum.

It can be daunting to try to meet the challenges of linguistic diversity, especially if you are working in isolation. Be assured that there are many tools and understandings that can help you meet the needs of the second language students with whom you interact on a daily basis. These strategies can improve the academic achievement of all students and also provide a sense of satisfaction and accomplishment at having truly made a difference in students' lives. What you do day to day does make a difference. For us, and for many of you, this opportunity to make a difference is why we went into teaching in the first place.

A school-wide collaborative approach to your community of learners is your key to success. It is not up to you alone. All school personnel should assume shared responsibility for the components necessary for the academic success of second language learners and together participate as decision makers in school-wide efforts. Remember that as a teacher you have the most control over what you do in the classroom on a daily basis. Principals' understandings of second language issues and of effective leadership are critical in orchestrating educationally sound and collaborative settings in which second language learners can succeed. In addition, district administrators constitute an essential element in these efforts. Such collaborative approaches can often be built through a concerted restructuring or reform process (Miramontes et al., 1997).

What Can Be Done?

There are many steps that can be taken to address the needs of a linguistically diverse student body. What follows are our perspectives on the elements needed to create schools where teachers, administrators, parents, and community members can come together in a joint effort to build academic success.

We believe that everyone has a role in guaranteeing the success of linguistically and culturally diverse students. Our recommendations include things that all educators can do in big and small ways, every day, in every classroom, in every school, and in every district. They are equally applicable in schools where instruction is all in English as well as in those schools able to incorporate students' first language in the delivery of the curriculum. They take into account both the larger political context and the need for appropriate instructional strategies on a daily basis. Each of these is elaborated upon in the following section.

THINGS EVERY TEACHER CAN DO

- *Focus on equity and creating a climate of belonging for all students.*

- *Examine your beliefs regarding an academically literate person.*

- *Organize instruction to build on the relationship between students' learning in their first and second languages and value what students bring with them from home.*

- *Gather data about the learners' prior language and literacy experiences.*

- *Be conscious of the need to group and regroup students during their instructional day to account for their varying language proficiencies.*

- *Make a firm commitment to standards-based instruction that is focused on, and driven by, the needs of students.*

- *Analyze instructional activities to account and adjust for language proficiency.*

- *Pay attention to the differences in the way literacy develops through first and second languages.*

- *Use the physical environment to help create meaning-based instruction.*

- *Utilize strategies that will increase comprehension and that provide opportunities for interaction among the students.*

---

1. Focus on Equity and Creating a Climate of Belonging for All Students

Part of the challenge of working in linguistically diverse schools is how to accommodate the various groups that such schools bring together. When asked what they most need to meet this challenge, teachers invariably reply "instructional strategies." However, all the best strategies will likely be insufficient if they are employed in a setting where students do not feel valued or have the confidence that they can succeed. The need to create a positive affective climate where the home language and culture of every student is valued cannot be underestimated. Sonia Nieto (1999) proposes that the nature of teacher–student relationships is central to student learning.

> The way students are thought about and treated by society and consequently by the schools they attend and the educators who teach them is fundamental in creating academic success or failure. (p. 167)

Researchers (Lucas, Henze, & Donato, 1990) have also found that in schools experiencing success with language-minority students:

- Value is placed on the students' languages and cultures.
- High academic expectations are communicated to language-minority students.
- School leaders make the education of language-minority students a priority.
- Parents of language-minority students are encouraged to become involved in their children's education.
- School staff members share a strong commitment to empower language-minority students through education.

These understandings about social context coincide with one of the most fundamental conditions for fostering second language acquisition a safe, caring and encouraging environment (Krashen, 1985; Stevick, 1976, 1982). Second language learners experience tremendous stress resulting from the difficult and sometimes embarrassing task of learning another language. Their language learning is enhanced when affective factors are addressed and when they find themselves in settings that allow them to develop a sense of security. Simply put, second language learners are more likely to succeed when their teachers create safe, caring environments that promote risk-taking.

Building a positive climate is relatively easy when teachers and students are from similar backgrounds and share common experiences and expectations. However, the often strong differences among the communities and teachers that comprise linguistically diverse schools present additional challenges in creating this positive climate. These differences may even reflect differing views of what it means to provide an equitable education. We concur with Nieto's suggestions that school reform efforts that can substantially improve student learning are proactively antiracist and antibias in their orientation. Examining our biases and the biases of those around us helps us create environments in which all students are seen as having talents and strengths that can enhance both their education and the community in general. In addition, developing an understanding and genuine respect for the important role family and culture play in each of our lives helps teachers recognize the importance of these elements in the lives of their students.

No matter what their cultural or linguistic background, all teachers have a role in building academic success for all students. It is undeniably impor-

tant that students have role models from their own cultural backgrounds—
a typical condition for mainstream, middle class white students (Gordon,
Della Piana, & Keleher, 2000; SSCORE, 2004). It is equally important for
students to see that people from backgrounds different from their own can
be role models as well. Just as teachers of color should be seen as models
for all of their students, white teachers can certainly be models of what it is
to be anti-racist, to embrace diversity, and to advocate for the equitable
treatment of all students.

In developing our own classrooms, each of us will reflect our personal
beliefs about students and learning. These beliefs should not go unexamined. Consider what it means that at their core, successful schools in linguistically diverse settings focus on both content and context. The following are some questions for you to ponder.

- How do you build an understanding of, and respect for, diversity into
  your practice?
- How do you provide fair and equitable opportunities where each student has the best chance of learning?
- How will your personal beliefs affect how you interpret the recommendations in this book?
- How might a colleague approach this differently?
- What else do you need to know about your students that will help you
  to help them grow and blossom?
- What do the answers to these questions mean to you, your students,
  and your school community?
- What kind of active steps can you take to create a strong educational
  program based on these understandings?

What Can I Do to Focus on Equity and Create a Climate of Belonging?
As you think about these questions remember that there is not one right
thing to do. There are countless ways to act on these understandings and
create a warm and safe learning environment. Among the actions to take
are:

- Utilize materials that acknowledge students' cultures and help them
  feel like they belong in your classroom.
- Demonstrate a value for students' ability to use two languages.
- Reach out and bring community members (carpenters, mechanics,
  business owners, etc.) into the school as partners in building a sense

of community, contributing to instruction, and supporting the school in providing for all the needs of its students.

- Send a unified message from the school encouraging immigrant parents and family members to interact and communicate with their children in their strongest language (usually not English).

Whatever actions you take should be grounded in the needs of your own students and your own school community.

2. Examine Your Beliefs Regarding an Academically Literate Person

Second language learners of English are students who live in bilingual worlds. They are called on daily to use two languages as tools for interaction, for communication, for negotiating daily activities, and for learning. Too often, however, educators overlook the fact that whether or not second language learners receive primary language instruction in school, they are always learning through both their languages. Besides school learning, they are learning from parents, grandparents, and other family and community members. Many of the students are also learning in their first language through television, radio, and other media. If utilized effectively, all of this can support their academic development in school. Understanding primary language inputs and interactions is critical to creating a sound instructional program for the students.

As reflected in the public arguments, knowledge in a language other than English is often discounted or ignored, as we forget that all over the world people are successfully engaged in government, education, science, religion, politics, and so forth, without ever speaking a word of English.

What Constitutes Academic Proficiency? When discussing academic proficiency, it is important to reflect on the nature of academic learning, the role language plays in children's development and what we are trying to accomplish with students. Think about the attributes of successful people around the world who are academically well prepared and highly literate. Certainly they can read and write well. They are critical thinkers and problem solvers as demonstrated by their ability to: make predictions or come up with creative solutions, differentiate fact from opinion, infer causes, suggest alternative explanations, and so on. They might also have a sense of fairness, a commitment to helping others and/or an appreciation of the arts. Although no single definition will satisfy everyone, whatever characteristics constitute your vision of this person, they should define true academic success and guide your work with all students.

For monolingual speakers of any language, becoming this literate academically competent person is accomplished solely through their first and only language. From infancy they not only learn language, but also how to use this language to think. When something new is learned it is added to a reservoir of concepts, schema, understandings, and skills developed through this first language. For their entire life they continue to add to and access their concepts only in their first language. Monolingual English speakers always use English to learn and communicate. Monolingual Thai speakers always use Thai to learn and communicate.

For those who by choice or by circumstance have the opportunity to develop more than one language, the pathway to academic literacy is more complex. In the beginning, one language is usually linked to development, bonding with parents, siblings, and community and learning to negotiate and communicate with others. As a second language is acquired, both languages become available to the learner as tools for adding to their knowledge base and thinking skills. Second language learners do not need to create a separate new reservoir of concepts. Once they know and understand something in one language or context, they can learn to express it in another. In the field of linguistics this is conceptualized as Common Underlying Proficiency—CUP (Cummins, 1979; Oller, 1980).

Second language learners generally begin by expressing what they already know in their first language with new words that they learn in their second. Listening to and understanding another language is easier than having to speak it. For second language learners of English, what they can understand in English will continue to be more advanced than what they can say in English until their English language proficiency catches up. As their overall English proficiency grows, learners will also be able to add more to their conceptual reservoir through English. In turn, they can then learn to express and deepen these new learnings in their first language. Hands on learning helps make those links. Students learning through two languages can be guided in how they can build on, or transfer, what they already know and are learning in one language to be able to extend what they can express in the other. This is why continued first language development is always beneficial to students.

As an example, consider students in U.S. schools who arrive here already having learned in Spanish about place value in math. They do not need to relearn the concept of place value to use it in math in English. They just need to learn how to express in English the knowledge they already have acquired in Spanish. As a part of this process the vocabulary and language structures for talking about place value in English needs to be developed.

The same process works for concepts that are more abstract. For example, the words *amistad, amicizia, amitié, freundschaft, vriendschap,* and friendship, all represent a common idea. Just as in the place value example, the meaning of *amistad* does not need to be relearned when it is relabeled as friendship, but the vocabulary needed to talk about it in a new language will need to be taught and practiced. The parameters of who can be friends, what friends do, and how friends communicate may well vary across cultures. Becoming exposed to and learning to understand the commonalties and differences of the nuances of ideas in different cultures is part of the enrichment of becoming bilingual.

The Advantages of Being Bilingual.   Being bilingual expands the definition of "academically competent." To be able to read, write, and think in two languages is more than the ability to do so separately in each one (Grosjean, 1989; Hornberger, 2000; Shannon & Shannon-Gutierrez, forthcoming). Research has demonstrated bilinguals' greater mental flexibility (Diaz, 1983; Hakuta, 1990; Lambert, 1977). Part of the advantage that accrues to bilinguals is the ability to compare and contrast their thinking across their two languages, something monolinguals of any language can't do. It also provides access to ways of thinking about any situation from more than one viewpoint. This ability to look at any situation or text through the lens of two languages can bring a whole new dimension to the understanding and appreciation of the nature of human existence and, especially, how it is reflected in the literature of different cultures.

The advantages of being academically bilingual can be developed for all children, including native English speakers. Unfortunately, these advantages seldom accrue to native English speakers in the United States because bilingualism is not generally valued or taken into account in the organization of public schools. This could change with vocal community support for schools that actively encourage learning through more than one language. This is why we view the presence of speakers of languages other than English as a gift. They bring us all the ability to see the world from multiple perspectives. They can also provide authentic opportunities for native English speakers to learn and communicate in another language. To value bilingualism does not diminish the importance of English. It does prompt us to try to foster all students' ability to use and maintain other languages in addition to English in whatever ways possible.

How are these understandings helpful in guiding teachers' planning of instruction? The transfer process can either be facilitated or hindered by the kind of instruction students receive and the kind of mediation their teachers provide (Bernhardt, 2003; Escamilla, 1993; Grant & Wong, 2003). If time were unlimited, it might not matter how carefully teachers planned. However, because we can only work with students for a limited number of hours in the school day, it makes sense to coordinate what happens across the day. Teachers can consciously plan in a way that capitalizes on the understanding that ideas, skills, and concepts learned in one language can be expressed in the other. In addition, by highlighting transfer in instruction, students can learn to pay attention to how what they know in one language can help their learning in the other. Instruction designed to take advantage of transfer recognizes that the concepts students have already acquired are not retaught—they are reinforced. It is precisely the differences between their expression in the two languages that must be explored. It is also important in organizing instruction to recognize that different strategies and approaches will be more or less successful depending on the setting and the language of instruction.

3. Organize Instruction to Build on the Relationship Between Students' Learning in Their First and Second Languages and Value What They Bring With Them From Home

As previously emphasized, to become academically proficient in a second language students need multiple opportunities to see, hear, and interact with new ideas, concepts, vocabulary, and language structures. In order to use all of their resources, students need to learn to transfer what they know to new situations as they also acquire new knowledge. This doesn't happen through translation, simply saying words twice, or explaining repeatedly in a language that is not understood. It does occur through careful planning.

The Importance of Making Connections.   In all kinds of programs connecting what students read and write about during literacy instruction with topics from the content areas will help provide these opportunities. In all-English programs, when teachers make intentional connections across settings and contexts, students are more likely to be able to build on what they have learned in one part of the day to understand what is happening in another. Chances increase that they will be able to repeatedly hear and practice new vocabulary, language structures, and concepts with which they must become fluent.

If two languages are being used in the students' instruction, teachers can also pay attention to coordinating what is taught in each language. Teachers can work together to purposefully mediate transfer of knowledge from one language to the other. For example, teachers can align instruction so students are working on common standards, and genres, and/or similar concepts at their level of proficiency in each language. They can read in their primary language about a topic they will encounter in English in another part of the day. Or, they can do an oral description in their second language of a visual image they have already been exposed to through their first language. As previously discussed, this does not mean simply translating nor are we suggesting that students repeat the same activities in each language. The essence of transfer is to expand topics from one language to the other, rather than merely restating the same thing in the other language.

Parents as Partners.   We take for granted that in the homes of native English speakers, parents reinforce instruction through their children's first language. Especially in all-English programs, it is important to proactively enlist the parents of second language learners to also help their children build background knowledge and schema through their first language. Based on the understanding of Common Underlying Proficiency and transfer, teachers can advocate that families consciously add to students' conceptual reservoir using the language they know best. They can do this by talking about school topics and discussing at home what students are learning about in school. We are not advocating that parents teach the curriculum at home. We are suggesting that parents can and should be asked to talk to their children in their primary language about whatever they are learning.

For example, if students are studying about natural disasters and the forces of nature, parents should not be expected to instruct their children in how the movement of tectonic plates causes earthquakes. They can, however, build background knowledge, schema, and visual imagery by talking about what they do know about earthquakes and how they know it. Have they, or anyone they know, ever been in an earthquake? What was it like? What would the family do in the case of an earthquake? What would be the worst thing about being in an earthquake? In this way students return to school with additional mental images and schemas that allow them to make more connections with what they are learning in school in either language (Gibbons, 1991, 2002; Harvey & Goudvis, 2000; Keene & Zimmerman, 1997). The entire school community will need to constantly reaffirm for parents that it will help their children's thinking and learning in English more if they talk about these ideas in their home language.

What Can I Do to Build on Students' Learning in Both Languages and to Value Their Homes?

- Recognize that learning in a language other than English contributes to overall academic proficiency.
- Try to determine, recognize, and use what students already know and understand about the topics of instruction.
- Make purposeful connections between what students do in different parts of their day and between what they know in each language.
- Inform parents about ongoing units of study and encourage them to use their first language to participate in their children's learning.

4. Gather Data About the Learners' Prior Language and Literacy Experiences

As we have discussed, in linguistically diverse settings the language background of the learners will significantly interface with the language of instruction. A successful plan, therefore, depends on having data about the learners, their language proficiency, and their academic performance. Teachers must determine who the learners are and what they bring to their instruction. Many teachers already use information about students' level of literacy or learning style to adjust their instruction. In linguistically diverse schools, language proficiency—what students understand and can express both in English and in their native language is an additional major factor that must also be taken into account in the planning process.

Second language learners inhabit a linguistic world in which they often know and can say some things in English but know and can say other things only in their home language. Therefore, these students present many language profiles that usually represent a different range of proficiency in each language. They may have greater strength in one language or the other depending on the topic under discussion. This is sometimes termed mixed dominance. For example, students who are in all English programs may continue to develop social language related to home and family in their first language, but may not have in that home language the vocabulary needed to express ideas related to content areas they are learning in school, in English. It is not that they don't understand the ideas, but that they have not been exposed to, or had practice with expressing the ideas in the other language.

Although mixed dominance occurs throughout the natural stages of language development, the term has, unfortunately, frequently been used to imply a state of stunted growth in which students will be stuck forever. This is an erroneous and shortsighted view. Successful movement through stages of proficiency, particularly academic language proficiency, will depend on teachers recognizing the learner's need for support in acquiring "missing" vocabulary and language structures. Being aware of words and constructions students are missing, presenting those words to them, and giving them opportunities to use them is the key to helping students move forward though these stages. Proactive support can help them to fill in language and knowledge gaps leading to fluency and academic proficiency.

Over time, students' knowledge and language proficiency will begin to balance out across languages if they are receiving instruction in both languages. However, especially if they are in all-English programs, many students will undergo what is called *subtractive bilingualism*. That is, they lose their first language and replace it with English. The advice to continue to support the primary language depends on students having retained their primary language at a high level in the home, or on sufficient previous schooling in the home language. It is important to understand that depending on where students are in this subtractive process some of them may no longer understand enough of the home language for recommendations regarding using the primary language at home to be completely effective. Support and respect for the primary language needs to continue, but the home language may no longer be a strong tool to support academic learning. The subtractive process can be stopped and schools can counteract this process by valuing the primary language and encouraging students and parents to continue to use it to build knowledge and vocabulary around new topics.

As already discussed, having a clear idea about former and present primary language use is a vital aspect of assessment and curriculum planning. The goal is to get a broader and more accurate picture of what students understand and can express with their full repertoire of language skills. In order to do so, wherever possible, academic and literacy skills should be evaluated in the students' primary language, as well as English, whether or not their primary language is used in formal instruction. This evaluation could include formal academic assessments, informal inventories, or even conversations with family members to document prior schooling and academic achievement levels. This information can be used to plan instruction that focuses on the transfer of knowledge already acquired, and to document the growth students make towards grade level benchmarks.

What Can I Do to Gather Data About the Learner's Language and Literacy Experiences?

- Ask questions and seek out information on what students were doing prior to your class.
- Identify someone who can help you with primary language assessment.
- Observe students interacting informally across different settings and in both languages, if possible.
- Observe students as they read, write, and interact in the classroom.
- Monitor students' development across listening, speaking, reading, writing, and understanding content.
- Check students' comprehension—have them tell you what they think they have learned and LISTEN CAREFULLY.

5. Be Conscious of the Need to Group and Regroup Students During Their Instructional Day, According to Their Language Proficiency

Any sound instructional design should purposefully plan for the grouping and regrouping (and regrouping again) of students. Although many other considerations go into forming groups for instruction, for second language learners the students' level of language proficiency needs to be a major indicator in helping guide teacher planning and their choice of strategies. In order to respond to the varying needs of second language learners it will be necessary to focus both on language and content development. This requires that students be given opportunities to focus deeply on the concepts, to practice the new language in a safe environment, and time to interact with native speakers.

It is not enough to ask, "What needs to be taught?" but also "What is the language background of the learners in front of the teacher?" and "Does the language of instruction match the language of the students?" In linguistically diverse schools, teachers can find themselves working with three different groups of students, each of which requires different strategies.

- Every student in front of the teacher is a native speaker of the language of instruction (Native Language Groups) or,
- The teacher is working with a group comprised of both native and second language speakers of the language of instruction (Heterogeneous Groups) or,
- All the students in front of the teacher are working in their second language (Second Language Groups).

Each setting provides necessary opportunities for the students, and places particular demands on their teachers.

Native Language Groups. The easiest and most comfortable instructional setting is when everyone—teacher and students—are fluent in the language of instruction. Working through the first language is the quickest avenue to academic development. When students work in their primary language, they can most easily access their conceptual understandings and background knowledge and teachers can employ a wide variety of strategies. Teacher education programs prepare teachers for this setting for native English-speakers who receive primary language instruction for nearly all of their schooling. They have the advantage of always being able to go deep into concepts, easily work on higher order thinking skills and make use of the full range of text materials available.

The fact that primary language instruction facilitates academic development is why proponents of bilingual education advocate for periods of time when second language students can work in their first language. A balance is needed because if second language learners spend their whole day learning only in their first language, they will not have the opportunity to learn a second language.

Heterogeneous Groups of First and Second Language Learners. As increasing numbers of second language learners attend U.S. schools, teachers often find themselves working with groups composed of both native and second language learners of English. When working with these heterogeneous language groups, the challenge for the teacher is to provide instruction that is both comprehensible to the second language learners and sufficiently challenging for the native speakers. Especially when teachers' prior experiences have been to work only with native English speakers where everybody understands the language, it is easy to forget the language demands of the activities. If teachers use strategies that are geared to the needs of the native speakers, some aspects of the instruction may be beyond the grasp of many second language learners and the group that is least proficient may be left out completely.

It is particularly important to understand the challenges of heterogeneous language grouping because this is the setting in which the vast majority of second language learners of English find themselves most of the time. Working in a heterogeneous language group can both provide and restrict opportunities. Such language groups can provide second language learners with many opportunities for "authentic" communication in English not available in other settings. On the other hand, second language learners' need for extra practice with vocabulary, sentence structures, and meaning cannot be satisfied if they are always in a group with native speakers. When most of the group is actively participating, teachers may be reluctant to slow down or stop to explain concepts and vocabulary in depth to a small group of students or not even realize that they need to do so.

Even when second language learners can understand their lessons in the heterogeneous group, attempts to speak English are frequently thwarted by the more proficient native English speakers who easily out compete them for the floor in whole group question and answer sessions and discussion groups. Staying in heterogeneous language groups all day also means second language learners won't be able to take advantage of time that would be spent in the primary language although such instruction would support their academic development by allowing students to go deeper into literacy and conceptual understandings.

Second Language Groups.   The third and very necessary grouping is where teachers are working only with second language learners. In this setting it will be obvious that students might not understand all of their instruction and it is more likely that teachers will recognize their need to use strategies to make instruction more understandable. The advantage for the students working in such groups is that they can focus on their English language learning needs without having to complete with students who are already proficient in English, and they can work on aspects of language not needed by native speakers. In this way they can feel more relaxed and comfortable taking chances and making mistakes and be better able to respond to their instruction. The sense of security they feel can lead to faster progress and to the formation of powerful and important relations with both school personnel and their peers. Any ESL teacher can attest to the special bonds that are built in their classrooms, both among the students and between the students and teacher.

One challenge in a second language setting is making sure the richness of the full curriculum is available to the students. There is a danger that teachers will overcompensate for students' lack of language proficiency by focusing so much on language that they miss important parts of the academic curriculum. If their teachers are trained only as language teachers, students' access to the big ideas and concepts of the academic curriculum may be limited. If content teachers are not properly trained in strategies for teaching students in their second language, they may begin to water down the curriculum to make it more accessible instead of working to make challenging concepts understandable.

Always being in any one of these three groups limits students' opportunities. In the case of always being in special classes for second language learners, the problem is that their chances to hear from and use English with native models in an academic setting will be severely limited. And again, if students are always working in their second language, they will miss valuable opportunities to build their literacy skills, content, and conceptual knowledge through their first language.

Proficiency in two languages can also be a goal for native English speakers and these understandings also apply to programs where the goal is for native English speakers to become fluent in a second language. In addition to the primary language instruction English speakers already receive, they will need to have time to practice their second language with native speakers of the other language as well as a time when they can work apart, focusing on their special needs as second language learners.

Which is the best grouping? The answer is that in a linguistically diverse setting no one grouping is best and *each* contributes to academic success, because what can be accomplished best in each grouping differs. In programs that use the primary language, each of these three different groupings needs to be part of students' instructional day. In any English-only setting, at a minimum, both homogeneous second language and heterogeneous grouping must be part of daily instruction and efforts should be made to encourage primary language use outside of school.

Careful planning will ensure consistency, a critical aspect of second language instruction. It does not necessarily require revamping the entire schedule to accommodate the three instructional groupings and the important understandings they embody. For example, in addition to regular daily ESL time, it may be possible during the course of a content or literacy lesson to pull together a small group of students to provide extra practice with new vocabulary or to use the primary language to go in depth on the concepts under study. Any school-wide plan will need to organize the adult human resources to allow for this grouping and regrouping of students.

What Can I Do to Implement This Idea of Grouping and Regrouping?

- Use student work, especially writing, to identify students with similar language needs and plan mini-lessons accordingly.
- Collaborate with other teachers to coordinate scheduling so that it is possible to group students across classrooms for specialized opportunities.
- Always ask yourself:

  What opportunities are afforded by each of the three groupings—native language, heterogeneous, and all second language groups—for the development of an academically competent or literate person?

  What constraints does each setting impose on this academic development?

  What are the most appropriate strategies to use in each setting to best meet the needs of the students represented?

6. Make a Firm Commitment to Standards-Based Instruction That Is Focused on, and Driven by, the Needs of Students

In schools with second language learners, there is a tendency to see the "real" curriculum as the mainstream native English curriculum. In this view something else other than the real or important learning is happening in ESL or bilingual programs. This should not be the case. No matter in what program students find themselves, a common curriculum should guide the planning for all learners in a grade level, content area, school, or district. The strategies that teachers use to deliver the curriculum in a comprehensible fashion and how they link to students' background knowledge are what make the information accessible to all students.

The promise of authentic standards based instruction is that all students will have access to, and experience success with the academic curriculum. Instruction should be challenging, relevant, and foster the kinds of critical thinking and problem solving capabilities that characterize an academically competent literate person. Instruction should address the broad understandings and skills that all students should know and possess. This does not mean all children should be on the same page of the social studies textbook on the same day. Nor does it mean that their learning can be accurately assessed with a statewide high stakes multiple-choice test. It does

mean recognizing that there is a body of knowledge in every field represented by ways of thinking, fundamental concepts, big ideas, and a certain
skill set that should guide planning and instruction.

Fundamental concepts are those big ideas from the content areas that
transcend particular units. For example, "The environment—created and
shaped by natural forces or modified by humans, shapes the life forms that
occupy it." Or "All forms of life depend on food, water, shelter, and space
in a suitable arrangement" (Council for Environmental Education, 2001,
p. 459). These kinds of fundamental ideas can be reflected in curriculum
from kindergarten through doctoral studies. The principle remains the
same, whereas the depth of understanding and the level of language and
literacy skills through which individuals express those understandings will
vary. Importantly, this body of knowledge can be learned through any language a student speaks and can understand.

Varying Instructional Approaches.   Operating on the principle that all
students have the right of equal access to the knowledge embodied in the
curriculum implies that teachers will have to *differentiate* instruction to assure success (Gardner, 1993; Gregory & Chapman, 2002; Tomlinson,
1999, 2001). It is not sufficient to employ a one-dimensional instructional
approach based on a single source of information. Unfortunately, it is still
all too common that teachers conduct lectures, have students read the
grade level textbook chosen for the topic or subject, and then answer questions at the end of the chapter as their only mode of instruction. If the goal
is to assure that all students experience success with the material, however, teachers must employ multiple teaching strategies that address different learning styles, language proficiencies, and levels of literacy development. It will be necessary to utilize materials and learning activities to
teach about the topics at a range of reading levels. The thread that holds
the plan together are the standards, the big ideas, and the concepts that
need to be learned by all.

In a standards-based approach, there is a predictable sequence of curriculum planning that begins with the end in mind. Very briefly,[1] you must
identify the outcomes you expect as a result of your instruction by asking,
"What should students know?" At the same time, you identify the skills
that will be acquired by asking: "What should students be able to do as a
result of my instruction?" You then determine how you will know whether

---

[1]This admittedly is a very truncated description of standards-based instruction. The bibliography
includes a number of excellent resources for such planning (e.g., Jacobs, 1997; Laturnau, 2002;
Tomlinson, 1999, 2001; Wiggins & McTighe, 1999).

students have accomplished your objectives by deciding what formative and summative assessments will be used. Finally, you plan the learning experiences that will constitute your instruction and ensure that you reach your goals. These goals should always lead students to new understandings and learnings.

In successful standards-based classrooms, teachers are like conductors who orchestrate instruction, employing a variety of methods and modalities. They do whatever it takes to reach the whole class. The teacher/artist brings together knowledge of the learner, the situation, the strategies and techniques most needed for success and blends these into a comprehensive approach to daily instruction (DePorter, Reardon, & Singer-Nourie, 1999). Perhaps one of the most rewarding things about teaching second language learners and other learners who really need a good teacher's talents is having the opportunity to know the meaning of this art of teaching.

What Can I Do to Implement Standards-Based Instruction?

- Familiarize yourself with any standards for your grade level or content area that have been adopted in your school district, or by the professional organization that represents your area of specialty.
- Work with colleagues to determine clear benchmarks to guide instruction.
- Identify and display the enduring understandings, big ideas, and vocabulary of whatever you are teaching and highlight them in instruction.
- Identify before each unit key questions that students will be able to answer at the end. Post them. Refer to them as lessons develop and teach the concepts.
- Provide students with multiple avenues for learning about, interacting with and displaying their knowledge about the topics of instruction.

7. Analyze Your Instructional Activities to Account for Language Proficiency

Part of meeting the challenge of linguistic diversity is accounting for both the language as well as the content demands of instructional activities. When planning for native English speakers, it is easy to overlook how every activity depends on certain linguistic competencies, understandings, and vocabulary knowledge. Developing English proficiency for native speakers is the result of their years of learning and interacting with the language. This use of language reflects complex levels of development from early childhood to school age. Because we take language for granted, we often assume that second language learners also understand the content and are able to talk freely about it.

Second language learners have to learn both the content and learn the words and modes of expression for that content. Each of these aspects calls for distinct strategies that both require planning (Echevarria & Short, 2004). All too often, the complexity of language development for second language learners is boiled down to a focus on vocabulary alone and is equated with learning a list of new words. It is not necessary to be an ESL teacher to figure out the language demands of your instruction. You can begin by simply examining the activities you have chosen for students to do and ask, "What are the features of language that students need to understand and be able to use in order to accomplish this activity successfully?"

Here is an example: Students in a fourth grade class have done investigative research papers on various explorers. Because of the range of language proficiencies in the classroom, some students required extensive support in gathering and reading information. Others received extra support in learning the vocabulary and sorting out important information for their writing, others needed help in writing out the information. Now that the papers are written, the culminating activity chosen will require students to participate in a kind of living museum where students take on the role of their explorer ready to answer questions about themselves based on their research. One student's research report says:

> *Marco Polo was one of the most important explorers of the 13th century. He was born in the year 1254. His father and his uncle asked him to join them on their world adventures.*

At the most basic level, to adjust for the living museum, the student will need to be prepared to say

> ***My name is*** *Marco Polo.* ***I am*** *one of the most important explorers of the 13th century.* ***I was*** *born in the year 1254.* ***My*** *father and* ***my*** *uncle asked* ***me*** *to join them on their world adventures.*

The initial report is written in the third person. To become the explorer and answer questions, the student will have to switch to the first person. This requires changes in verbs, pronouns, and possessives. Once prompted with an example, most native English speakers will automatically make the changes to shift to the first person. Second language learners, on the other hand, may or may not recognize the need to make the shift. Even if they do, they may still lack the linguistic knowledge necessary to do so, which makes the activity much more challenging for them.

This example represents a relatively straightforward change. Academic work usually embodies more complicated structures. Think about the demands of a debate where students not only have to know the content of the subject, but also the very strict rules of format. Think now about participating in the Science Fair where students need to explain their hypotheses, describe their data collection methods, report out on the data and explain their conclusions. In such a setting, they will also be required to understand questions asked of them and spontaneously respond. Each step of this process demands particular facility with the structures of the language as well as the content of the science experiment. Living museums, debates, science fairs—just about any activity—can be perfectly appropriate for second language learners. It will be necessary to provide them with time to prepare—time to practice the structures and grammar of English—as well as guidance in how to express this information appropriately in English. This is not the sole responsibility of ESL or bilingual teachers. It needs to be accounted for in everyone's instructional planning. Commercially available programs can proved a framework and guidance for language focused instruction, but this is not to advocate for a lock step grammar program. To the contrary it means basing the particulars of language instruction on the needs of the students. Any instruction in the structure of language should be based on the real life demands of the content area and literacy curriculum.

What Can I Do to Account for the Language Demands of My Instruction?

- Review the scope and sequence of several comprehensive ESL series in order to familiarize yourself with how they describe both the functions of language, as well as the basics of English grammar and structure.

- Analyze your activities to identify features of language, such as grammar, functions, and vocabulary that will need additional instruction.

- Provide the time for second language learners to work on these aspects of academic language both orally and in writing.

8. Be Conscious of the Differences in the Way Literacy Develops Through First and Second Languages

Most immigrant children in this country are in all-English programs. This means that their formal schooling happens only through their second language, whereas their early learning has been in a different language. Appropriate instruction for this different type of learner takes careful planning and recognizes that strategies defined as "best practice" for students learning in their first language may have limited success when they are used with second language learners (Bernhardt, 2003; Escamilla, 1993; Grant & Wong, 2003). Because most teachers have only been prepared to work with monolingual English speakers learning in English (a mismatch with many of their students) little thought is usually given to how the strategies depend on certain funds of ideas and words to express them. Especially when teachers have experienced success working with native speakers, they can easily feel that they just need to slightly adjust what they are doing to meet the needs of second language learners. However, minor adjustments may not be enough for any particular practice to work well for students learning through their second language. Teachers must carefully consider that second language students will require much more extensive attention to language development than is required for native speakers.

The fundamental aspects of good literacy instruction hold true across languages. Learning strategies such as knowing and using the different cueing systems, reading for meaning versus decoding, reading and writing to students, with students, and by students; gradual release of responsibility from the teacher to the learner are all part of sound instruction (Au, Carrol, & Scheu, 2001; Keene & Zimmerman, 1997; Routman, 2003). The ultimate goal is for students to comprehend meaning. Every comprehension strategy depends on a fund of concepts, vocabulary, and grammatical knowledge that will help readers make sense of the text in front of them.

By focusing on the commonalties instead of the differences in literacy instruction across two languages, teachers too often miss critical aspects of what second language readers need. For second language learners, especially those learning to read solely through their second language, additional steps need to be taken before students can handle text in the same way as native speakers. Although second language readers might be able to decode English text, they might not have the background to bring meaning to it. It is especially important that literacy instruction for students learning in their second language reflect teachers' understanding that comprehension is key. In order to comprehend text, learners need to have a strong command of the concepts, words, and language structures utilized in the reading material. It will be easier to learn to read and derive meaning when students already have had practice in talking about and understanding the big ideas and vocabulary represented in the text.

Let's take, for example, Guided Reading, an integral part of a balanced approach to literacy instruction (Fountas & Pinnel, 1996; Routman, 2003). Guided Reading is time in the instructional day when teachers work with small groups of students to focus on strategies that will assist the learners at their level of reading proficiency. In our experience, the implementation of Guided Reading has, more often than not, become synonymous with the use of leveled texts in a particular sequence of activities moving each day from book to book within one level until students are ready for the next. One step in this process is "the picture walk" where the teacher and students look at each page of the book and talk about the text through the pictures before reading. For native speakers this readily stimulates connections and generates words students are likely to encounter in the text.

To modify for second language learners teachers tell us that they "extend the picture walk" by naming more of the objects in the pictures. If there are only one or two unfamiliar words in the whole text, this small adjustment may be effective. When each page represents several new words and possibly an unfamiliar context, however, spending just a few extra minutes extending the picture walk may not tap into what students know and are able to talk about in English. This becomes especially problematic when Guided Reading groups are composed of both native and second language speakers who may be reading the same level text for very different reasons. An extended picture walk may not allow second language learners sufficient time to generate the language used to represent the ideas and build the vocabulary, concepts, and schema needed to successfully comprehend the text in English. It will take much more to prepare them for the text. The pictures may first need to be the vehicle for introducing words and even concepts they have never used before. It may take several days for second language learners to activate the necessary background knowledge and be able to express it confidently in English.

Guided Reading and leveled books can certainly have a place in the literacy instruction of second language learners. One solution is to conduct guided reading activities in groups composed of students with similar language proficiency backgrounds. For example, if Guided Reading occurs during a time when second language learners are working together, it is much easier to allow for the kinds of extended language preparation that will be needed. This would make it possible as part of the Guiding Reading time, for example, to first talk in depth about and/or develop a language experience story based on the pictures and big ideas represented in the books, experiences that may not be necessary for native English speakers. It may also be more efficacious to use several books at different levels around a common theme so that students have a chance to master both the ideas represented and the words used to express them.

These recommendations also don't mean that second language learners shouldn't be doing a lot of reading. Research points to the great benefits in language development from reading (Fay & Whaley, 2004; Franklin, 1999; Krashen, 2002, 2004). A principal distinction is the way in which text is created, used, and built on. When students are learning to read in a second language, building background knowledge, schema, and language through extensive sheltering and oral practice that goes with it first will enhance reading ability. The names of the letters of the alphabet are far less important for them at the beginning stages of reading than developing a repertoire of language, vocabulary, and concepts in the second language that will allow them to understand what they are reading about.

What Can I Do to Reflect These Understandings About Literacy Development?

- Consider the need to develop meaning before interacting with text.
- Become acquainted with the ways literacy is used daily in the homes of your students.
- Use text to represent ideas and concepts that students understand and can talk about.
- Seek materials on every topic at a range of reading levels and complexity.
- Incorporate language experience approaches.
- Make conscious connections between the big ideas from the content areas and the things that students will read and write about during literacy instruction.

9. Use the Physical Environment to Help Create Meaning-Based Instruction

The most basic need of second language learners is to derive meaning from their instruction. Although a standards-based approach provides a strong context, it does not a guarantee that students will experience success. An important aspect of delivering meaning-based instruction in a linguistically diverse environment is how you use the physical space in the room. To maximize comprehensibility, the physical space should be designed to always tie together meaning and text. You should avoid "decorating" your classroom and, instead, utilize every inch of the room as a resource for students in their independent work.

In any good classroom it should be apparent to students from the physical environment the topics they are learning about, the expectations for their behavior, and the main guidelines for how to accomplish their work. Many teachers embrace the understanding that students thrive in a print rich environment. In a typical elementary classroom you might find the schedule for the day, a list of jobs, rules for writers workshop or steps in the writing cycle, a list of the standards and a place to display students' work. In such environments good readers of the language will be able to make use of the print that surrounds them to know what to do. Unfortunately, "print rich" does not always equal "meaningful" if students can't understand what the print says. Even if second language learners are able to decode the print, they still may not be able to derive any meaning from what is posted.

In a school with second language learners, simply putting things up in writing is not sufficient to make them comprehensible. Some additional steps are necessary in order to make print rich environments useful and comprehensible to second language learners. To get an idea of this, think of your classroom and the text that is on the walls. Now imagine that this text is in a language with a completely different writing system—Chinese, Arabic, Lao, Hebrew, Cyrillic, and so on. Would you have any clues as to the topics of instruction or the expectations for work in that area of the room? Would you be able to distinguish a science center from a math center, from a list of Writer's Workshop strategies, from the rules for staying safe during a severe weather disturbance? If so, how? If not, why not?

One response to the previous advice is to fill the walls with pictures. Although this may make ideas and themes more visible, in and of itself it will do little to further students' understandings or literacy development. The key in a linguistically diverse environment is to always mediate understanding with both text and visual images. Text that appears on the walls should be contextualized with pictures, and supported with examples tied to the big ideas of instruction. All the pictures and text should be reviewed by the teacher periodically with links made to the important topics being studied. Any pictures and visual images can be mediated by posing questions and adding text that is related to their content. In this way, you will increase the likelihood that all students can use the physical environment as a source for independent learning. Although some think that to modify instruction to account for understandings of language acquisition is an additional burden, in reality, many adaptations intended for second language learners will enhance instruction for all students. These strategies will be more productive when employed in the context of an integrated curriculum and/or thematic units that consciously account for oral language development in all aspects of instruction.

What Can I Do to Enhance the Physical Environment?

- Focus on the big ideas of instruction and use multiple modalities to teach them.
- Identify and utilize visual images, gestures, and objects to represent the big ideas in all content areas.
- Use questions and statements to label the room and the work displayed.
- Read labels with students and relate them to the pictures and topics.

10. Utilize Strategies That Will Increase Comprehension and Provide Opportunities for Interaction

There are many, many strategies teachers can use to make instruction more accessible to their students. In the section entitled "Strategies for Second Language Instruction," the bibliography contains an extensive list of references regarding instructional strategies that are useful for second language learners. Much of the advice in those volumes is embodied in two major principles: (1) provide comprehensible input and (2) create opportunities for practice and interaction. The first principle implies that you must do whatever is necessary to make the lesson accessible. Always ask yourself: How can I make the instruction and the materials I am using understandable? How do I know students really understand the material?

The second principle regarding constant opportunities for student interaction and talk is based on the understanding that in order to become fluent in a language, you have to practice—A LOT. In learning a language, words and phrases need to be heard and repeated often and in a variety of contexts before they are mastered and become part of the students' own vocabulary. You need to provide students with many opportunities to talk aloud and converse with others regarding instruction.

What Can I Do to Increase Comprehension and Provide Opportunities for Interaction?

- Utilize hands-on activities, cooperative grouping strategies, and assign peers, mentors, and buddies to allow for maximum student participation.
- Use pictures, models, graphs, diagrams, charts, graphic organizers, and so forth to organize information and to elicit student talk.
- As concepts are initially being learned, place more emphasis on students' understanding of the big ideas from content-area instruction and less on how they express that knowledge.
- After students know the concepts, help them develop the language to fully express them in English.
- Monitor and encourage each student to participate orally in activities, model repeatedly when necessary. Model language for students and help them to practice it before requiring them to use it on their own.
- Elevate oral language practice by providing constant opportunities for interaction through increased student talk and decreased teacher talk.
- Remember that any question asked of the whole group can be answered first in partners—"Turn and talk to your neighbor about. . . ."

SUMMARY AND FINAL COMMENTS

In order to hold second language learners and native speakers to the same high expectations, instruction in linguistically diverse schools needs to be organized to allow students to grow in all the dimensions of academic development. Our advice: Collaborate with professional colleagues to create a flexible structure that allows for shared responsibility. Communication and collaboration among the adults in a linguistically diverse school is absolutely essential. All of this section's recommendations will be easier to follow when you incorporate them into a group effort.

Schools seeking improvement should begin by carefully analyzing the resources and expertise within a building or district. In any school where improvement is the goal, the question before the entire staff should be:

"How can we best organize ourselves and our resources to meet the needs of *all* students?" (Miramontes et al., 1997). Remember to take note of the things you already do in each area and consider what next step might be taken.

The kinds of discussions that should take place as part of a total plan for meeting the needs of the students happen best when educators take a school-wide perspective on meeting students' needs. Team planning and team teaching are ideal. Although the nature of the teaming and articulation will change depending on whether you work at the elementary or secondary level, in all schools consistency and predictability can be increased. This can be accomplished by articulating things such as guiding questions, basic elements of instruction, benchmarks and criteria, essential understandings, learning strategies, themes, topics, and genres across contexts and languages and grade levels. You might, for example, work in grade level teams where you could agree on the topics and common timeline for the social studies and science curricula.

Or you might work as a department to identify skills and understandings that bridge the various classes related to the subject matter. For example, all the science teachers in a building could agree on a common way of talking about and representing visually the steps and concepts embodied in the scientific method that transcend any particular area of science. That way students don't need to learn a new system in every classroom, but rather can concentrate on the important information related to the more abstract ideas in instruction.

Any conversation about instruction should also address how students can be grouped and regrouped among teams of adults to assure that they get to work in different ways on different aspects of language and conceptual development across their day. Although these recommendations require initial time and planning, they can be applied to any classroom, grade level, subject area or school, across all types of programs and settings.

Seek out professional development that brings all these understandings together and responds to linguistic diversity as a central feature. It is the range of student needs represented in the building that should guide the planning. The goal should be to create a system based on these needs rather than trying to make students adapt to a system designed for native speakers alone. Working together with colleagues, armed with knowledge and buoyed by the conviction that you can make a difference, you can significantly affect the opportunities provided and the positive outcomes afforded to your students.

EXERCISES FOR FURTHER REFLECTION

This final section provides suggestions for additional opportunities to interact with, and reflect on, teaching linguistically diverse students. These suggestions are grouped into three main categories that ask you to extend your thinking in different ways. They are intended to help you build your knowledge base and perhaps move beyond your comfort zone. They involve talking to people whose experiences may differ from your own, observing what goes on around you in relation to second language learners, as well as getting out and trying something new.

Get Other People's Perspectives

Interview a Second Language Teacher. There are many things you could ask about. Who are the students? What is the program like and what is its place in the total school environment? What role does the second language teacher have in the overall instructional plan of the school? How does this teacher see your role in relation to second language learners? What methods are most useful to this teacher and why? What frustrations does the teacher have and what are some ideas for how instruction for second language learners might be improved at the school? You can also ask about the satisfactions of the job and any special advantages there are to working with immigrant children.

Interview a Bilingual Teacher. All the questions just listed are applicable. In addition you can ask about the role of bilingualism in the total school environment and the differences between bilingual and monolingual education. What unique challenges does he or she face? How does he or she view relationships with students' families and the wider community? How did he or she became bilingual and how has being bilingual shaped his or her life?

Do a Mini Study on School Climate. Pay attention to the ways that the adults (and children) in your setting talk about immigrant students and their families. Keep a log for a week of any comments you hear in the lounge, in the parking lot, or in the community about these parents and their relationships with their children. Analyze the comments. What do they tell you about the way that second language learners and their families are viewed? Are immigrant parents viewed mostly positively or negatively in these conversations? Who do you see teachers conversing with after school and which parents stand alone? Do some people wait outside the classroom while others walk right in? What could you do to build on the positive and counteract the false stereotypes that may exist?

Interview the Parents of a Bilingual Child. Ask them about their hopes and aspirations for their children. Ask them to talk about bilingualism and what it means to them. Ask them how they feel about the program in which their child is enrolled and whether they think the program is helping their children to attain their goals. Ask them how to describe how they feel in the school setting.

Observe the World Around You

Observe How a Second Language Learner Uses Language. Choose a second language learner and shadow them across several different settings. In each setting notice with whom they interact, and particularly how students and teachers interact with each other. Does the student's use of language vary across settings, partners, topic, and/or languages? How do other people attempt to communicate with the student? What strategies does the learner use to make him or herself understood? Pay attention to how the students' demeanor changes (or doesn't) across settings. Try to find time to discuss these observations with the teacher.

Shadow Some Students Over the Course of a School Day. The purpose of this exercise is to see how students experience instruction in your program or school. Choose a grade and, if possible, identify three different students—a native English speaker, a second language learner who receives no primary language instruction (this may be all of them), and a second language learner who receives some primary language instruction. Document how each student spends the day. How long are they in a group in their first language with only native speakers of their language? How long are they in a group mixed with speakers of another language? Is this their first or second language? How much time are they in a group of just second language learners? Pay attention to whether the students' behavior changes in different settings. What changes do you observe?

Once you have an idea of how students experience their school day, examine whether the strategies used by teachers in each of these settings seem appropriate for the needs of the students they are teaching at that moment. Think about what this means for your own teaching.

Visit an Instructional Setting Where the Language Has an Alphabet You Can't Decode.   This setting may be a challenge to find depending on where you live. In some areas of the country you could visit a dual language program in Japanese, Chinese, or Arabic. You might be able to observe an after school or weekend class in Korean, Russian, or Chinese. In some places you might be able to visit a Hebrew Day School, and so on. Wherever you go, pay attention to how the physical environment helps you (or doesn't) to make sense of the instruction the students are receiving. What strategies would make this setting more comprehensible to you? What does this tell you about your own classroom's physical environment?

Make a Home Visit.   Focus on how parents perceive they are helping their children be successful in school. Pay attention to how different languages are used and represented in the environment. What possibilities and constraints exist in the student's home environment?

Do Something Yourself

Prepare and Teach a Short Lesson to a Second Language Learner. Choose a topic of interest to the learner and teach a short lesson. Focus on how you need to use language, other modes of communication—gestures, and so on. Analyze what worked and what didn't in terms of strategies, the use of text and/or getting the student to interact. You might want to teach the same lesson to a native speaker of English and note any differences between the two sessions.

Begin to Learn an Additional Language.   Even people who are already bilingual can forget or overlook the struggles, frustrations, embarrassments, and rewards that beginning second language learners experience. Try to learn more about a topic you are very familiar with in that language. Better yet study a topic about which you know very little and see how successful you are if you can only rely on input in that language. Pay attention to how you are feeling, reacting, and adapting. Most importantly, think about how this can inform your own teaching.

CONCLUSION

How do teachers learn how to teach? Typically we begin by imitating how we were taught, and to a lesser extent, trying to reflect the way in which we like to learn. The majority of you reading this book have had nearly all of your schooling in English. For most of you, this also means you received all your instruction in your first language. Teachers in the United States are still, by and large, being prepared exclusively to teach native English speakers in English. But the population of public schools is changing. The fact that you have read this book means that you have already begun a different path toward meeting the needs of all students.

We hope we have provided you with a fair account of the issues surrounding linguistic diversity and a view of the challenges and rewards that it brings. The art of teaching demands not that we don't make mistakes, but that we do our best to learn from them. We hope that the insights you have gained from our work and the work of countless teacher colleagues in the field will be the basis for ongoing reflective practice as you move through your teaching career. Know that each of you can make a difference for your students, especially when you take the time to get to know them, their families, and their communities. ¡Buena Suerte!

GLOSSARY OF TERMS

GENERAL TERMS ABOUT
LANGUAGE DEVELOPMENT

L1: First Language, Primary Language

L2: Second language—for some students English may actually be their 3rd or 4th language.

Proficiency: Level of listening, speaking, reading and/or writing abilities in any language

Dominance: Students usually have greater strengths in one language than the other.

Mixed Dominance: Having a range of skills across more than one language, usually according to the setting in which the language is used.

TERMS AND ACRONYMS USED
TO REFER TO THE LEARNERS

ELLs: English-Language Learners—Speakers of other languages who are learning English in school.

LEP: Limited English-Proficient—Term used in federal legislation—There are many objections to the term LEP because of its deficit orientation

FEP: Fully English-Proficient

NEP: Non English Proficient

FLEP: Formerly LEP—A potential category for classifying students—to account for students who have been redesignated as fluent in English, but were once classified as LEP.

PHLOTE: Primary or Home Language Other Than English. Terminology used in Office for Civil Rights Guidelines for students who live in homes where a language other than English is used for communication. All districts are supposed to identify these students, determine their level of English proficiency and provide special programming for those who are not yet proficient in English.

Bilingual: A person who speaks two languages. Misnomer when applied to students who are monolingual in a language other than English.

Monolingual: A person who only speaks one language. Misnomer when used to refer only to students who don't speak English without reference to the fact that most native English speakers are also monolinguals.

TERMS AND ACRONYMS APPLIED
TO PROGRAMS

Bilingual: A program that uses two languages for instruction. Misnomer when applied to a program that simply serves students who don't speak English.

English-Only: Submersion—Sink or Swim—All instruction is in English without making modifications to account for the needs of second language learners.

ESL: English as a Second Language—Term generally applied to programs and/or classes that focus specifically on language development. All good bilingual programs include an ESL component.

Immersion—Structured English Immersion: All instruction is in English and modifications are supposed to be made to account for the needs of second language learners.

ESL Pullout: Students are removed from the grade level classroom to receive instruction in the English language.

ESL Inclusion—Push-In ESL: Students receive instruction in English from an ESL teacher or tutor within the context of their grade level classroom.

Content-based ESL: Second language instruction that incorporates content area vocabulary and concepts as the medium for teaching the language.

Sheltered: Content instruction that is modified to meet the needs of second language learners. Teachers pay attention to the language demands of the assignments, texts and activities and modify their delivery to make instruction understandable using a variety of strategies, for example, visuals, hands-on, gestures, objects, graphic organizers. These are strategies that can be utilized by any teacher whether or not it is a formally designated sheltered class.

Dual Language: Another term for a program that uses two languages—sometimes used interchangeably with *Dual Immersion.*

Dual Immersion—Two-Way Immersion—Two-Way Bilingual: A bilingual program in which native speakers of both English and the target language learn both languages.

Early Exit—Transitional: First language is used for a short time as a bridge—as soon as basic literacy skills are acquired, students are moved to all-English instruction.

Late Exit—Maintenance—Developmental: Primary language continues to be utilized for academic and conceptual development even after students become proficient in English.

Newcomer programming: Programs for students who arrive in the upper grades (usually 4th and above). Can include processes for intake, assessment of language and academic background, and/or intensive language and academic instruction to prepare students to enter regular programs (ESL, Bilingual, or all English) at their grade level.

GENERAL TERMINOLOGY

OCR—Office for Civil Rights: Office within the U.S. Department of Justice whose role in education is to assure that all students receive equitable treatment in public schools.

Reclassification/Redesignation: Legal terms for the moment when a student's label is changed from LEP to FEP.

Redesignation Rate: The percentage of students who are reclassified in any given school year. (Should remain relatively constant whether or not new students enter the program).

Exit: To leave program services.

Transition: To shift the nature of instruction.

Transfer: Take what is known in one domain or language and apply it in another.

REFERENCES

We have tried to keep this list manageable. The first section contains references cited in this volume, followed by additional books and articles that we believe to be beneficial sources of information. There are many others as well.

Au, K. H., Carroll, J. H., & Scheu, J. A. (2001). *Balanced literacy instruction: A teacher's resource book* (2nd ed.). Norwood, MA: Christopher-Gordon.

Bernhardt, E. (2003). Challenges to reading research from a multilingual world. *Reading Research Quarterly, 38*(1), 112–117.

Chavez, L. (2003, Sept. 2). Schwarzenegger and the U.S. *Catholic Exchange.* Retrieved from: http://www. catholicexchange.com.

Collier, V. P. (1989). How long? A synthesis of research on academic achievement in a second language. *TESOL Quarterly, 23*(3), 507–531.

Collier, V. P. (1992). A synthesis of studies examining long term language minority student data on academic achievement. *Bilingual Research Journal, 16*(1&2), 187–212.

Council for Environmental Education. (2001). *Project Wild K–12 curriculum and activity guide.* Houston, TX.

Crawford, J. (2000). *At war with diversity: U.S. language policy in an age of anxiety.* Clevedon, UK: Multilingual Matters.

Cummins, J. (1979). Linguistic interdependence and the educational development of bilingual children. *Review of Educational Research, 49,* 222–251.

Cummins, J. (2000). *Language, power and pedagogy: Bilingual children in the crossfire.* Clevedon, UK: Multilingual Matters.

DePorter, B., Reardon, M., & Singer-Nourie, S. (1999). *Quantum teaching: Orchestrating student success.* Boston: Allyn & Bacon.

175

Diaz, R. M. (1983). The impact of bilingualism on cognitive development. In E. W. Gordon (Ed.), *Review of Research in Education, 10*, 23–54. Washington, DC: American Educational Research Association.

Echevarria, J., Vogt, M. E., & Short, D. H. (2004.) *Making content comprehensible for English language learners: The SIOP model.* Boston: Pearson Education.

English for the Children. (2004). www.onenation.org

Escamilla, K. (1993). Promoting biliteracy: Issues in promoting English literacy in students acquiring English. In J. Tinajero (Ed.), *The power of two languages: Literacy and biliteracy for Spanish-speaking students* (pp. 220–233). New York: Macmillan/McGraw Hill.

Franklin, E. (Ed.). (1999). *Reading and writing in more than one language: Lessons for teachers.* Alexandria, VA: Teachers of English to Speakers of Other Languages.

Fountas, I. C., & Pinnell, G. S. (1996). *Guided reading: Good first teaching for all children.* Portsmouth, NH: Heinemann.

Gardner, H. (1993). *Frames of mind: The theory of multiple intelligences.* New York: Basic Books.

Gibbons, P. (1991). *Learning to learn in a second language.* Portsmouth, NH: Heinemann.

Gibbons, P. (2002). *Scaffolding language, scaffolding learning: Teaching second language learners in the mainstream classroom.* Portsmouth, NH: Heinemann.

Gordon, R., Della Piana, L., & Keleher, T. (2000). *Facing the consequences: An examination of racial discrimination in U.S. public schools.* Applied Research Center. Retrieved from: www.arc.org/erase/FTC4demo.html.

Good, T. L., & Brophy, J. E. (2002). *Looking in classrooms* (9th ed.). Boston: Allyn & Bacon.

Grant, R. A., & Wong, S. D. (2003). Barriers to literacy for language-minority learners: An argument for change in the literacy education profession. *Journal of Adolescent & Adult Literacy, 46*(5), 386–394.

Gregory, G. H., & Chapman, C. (2002). *Differentiated instructional strategies: One size doesn't fit all.* Thousand Oaks, CA: Corwin Press.

Grosjean, F. (1989). Neurolinguists, beware! The bilingual is not two monolinguals in one person. *Brain and Language, 36*, 3–15.

Hakuta, K. (1990). Language and cognition in bilingual children. In A. Padilla, H. Fairchild, & C. Valadez (Eds.), *Bilingual education: Issues and strategies* (pp. 47–59). Newbury Park: Sage.

Harvey, S., & Goudvis, A. (2000). *Strategies that work: Teaching comprehension to enhance understanding.* York, ME: Stenhouse.

Hornberger, N. (2002). Multilingual language policies and the continua of biliteracy: An ecological approach. *Language Policy, 1*(1), 27–51.

Jacobs, H. H. (1997). *Mapping the big picture: Integrating curriculum and assessment K–12.* Alexandria, VA: Association for Supervision & Curriculum Development.

Keene, E., & Zimmerman, S. (1997). *Mosaic of thought: Teaching comprehension in a reader's workshop.* Portsmouth, NH: Heinemann.

Krashen, S. D. (1985). *Inquiries and insights.* Hayward, CA: Alemany Press.

Krashen, S. D. (2002). Three roles for reading for minority-language children. In G. Garcia (Ed.), *English learners: Reaching the highest level of English literacy.* International Reading Association.

Krashen, S. D. (2004). *The power of reading* (2nd ed.). Portsmouth, NH: Heinemann.

Lambert, W. E. (1977). The effects of bilingualism on the individual: Cognitive and socio-cultural consequences. In P. A. Hornby (Ed.), *Bilingualism: Psychological, social and educational implications*. New York: Academic Press.

Laturnau, J. (2002). *Standards based instruction for English language learners*. Pacific Resources for Education and Learning. Retrieved from: http://www.prel.org

Liston, D. P., & Zeichner, K. M. (1996). *Culture and teaching*. Mahwah, NJ: Lawrence Erlbaum Associates.

Lucas, T., Henze, R., & Donato, R. (1990). Promoting the success of Latino language-minority students: An exploratory study of six high schools. *Harvard Educational Review, 60*(3), 315–340.

Macias, R. (1997). *California LEP enrollment slows but continues to rise*. Linguistic Minority Research Institute, 7(1), 1–2.

Macias, R. (1998). *Summary Report of the survey of the states' limited English proficient students and available educational programs and services, 1996–1997*. Washington, DC: National Clearinghouse for Bilingual Education. Retrieved from: http://www. ncbe.gwu.edu/ncbepubs/seareports/96-97.

Maher, F. A., & Ward, J. V. (2002). *Gender and teaching*. Mahwah, NJ: Lawrence Erlbaum Associates.

McIntosh, P. (1988). *White privilege and male privilege: A personal account of coming to see correspondences through working in women's studies* (Working Paper No. 189). Wellesley, MA: Wellesley College, Center for Research on Women.

McPherson, S. S. (2000). *Lau v. Nichols: Bilingual education in public schools*. Berkeley Heights, NJ: Enslow Publishers.

Miramontes, O., Nadeau, A., & Commins, N. (1997). *Restructuring schools for linguistic diversity: Linking decision making to effective programs*. New York: Teachers College Press.

Mora, J. (2003). *California's demographics: Opportunity and challenge*. Retrieved from: http://www.coe.sdsu.edu/people/jmora/CAChallenges.

Nieto, S. (1999). *The light in their eyes: Creating multicultural learning communities*. Multicultural Education Series. New York: Teachers College Press.

No Child Left Behind Act of 2001. (2002). Pub. L. No. 107–110.

Oller, J. W., Jr. (1980). A language factor deeper than speech: More data and theory for bilingual assessment. In J. E. Alatis (Ed.), *Current issues in bilingual education* (pp. 14–30). Washington, DC: Georgetown University Press.

Paley, V. (1989). *White teacher*. Cambridge, MA: Harvard University Press.

Peregoy, S. F., & Boyle, O. F. (2002). *Reading, writing and learning in ESL: A resource book for K–12 teachers* (3rd ed.). New York: Addison Wesley Longman.

Rosenthal, R., & Jacobson, L. (2003). *Pygmalion in the classroom: Teacher expectation of pupil's intellectual development*. Crown House.

Routman, R. (2003). *Reading essentials: The specifics you need to teach reading well*. Portsmouth, NH: Heinemann.

Shannon, S. M., & Shannon-Gutiérrez, P. (in press). *Resisting the hegemony of English: Spanish and American sign language in the U.S.* Mahwah, NJ: Lawrence Erlbaum Associates.

SSCORE Southern California Consortium on Research in Education. (2004). *Teacher demographics*. Retrieved 7/31/04 from: http://www.sscore.org/2003/teachersandstaff/tchrdemmographics/tchrdemographics/shtml.

Stevick, E. W. (1976). *Memory, meaning and method: Some psychological perspectives on language learning.* Rowley, MA: Newbury House.

Stevick, E.W. (1982). *Teaching and learning languages.* New York: Cambridge University Press.

Tomlinson, C. (1999). *The differentiated classroom: Responding to the needs of all learners.* Alexandria, VA: Association for Supervision & Curriculum Development.

Tomlinson, C. (2001). *How to differentiate instruction in mixed ability classrooms* (2nd ed.). Alexandria, VA: Association for Supervision & Curriculum Development.

U.S. English. (2004). Retrieved from: http://usenglish/org/inc/offical/quotes.

Wiggins, G., & McTighe, J. (1999). *Understanding by design.* Alexandria, VA: Association for Supervision & Curriculum Development.

Wong Fillmore, L. (1989). When learning a second language means losing the first. *Early Childhood Research Quarterly, 6,* 323–347.

Bilingual Education/English-Only Debate

Baker, C. (2001). *Foundations of bilingual education and bilingualism* (3rd ed.). Clevedon, UK: Multilingual Matters Ltd.

Bali, V. (2001). Sink or swim: What happened to California's bilingual students after Proposition 227? *State Politics and Policy Quarterly,* 295–317.

Brisk, M. E. (1998). *Bilingual education: From compensatory to quality schooling.* Mahwah, NJ: Lawrence Erlbaum Associates.

Center for Equal Opportunity. (2004). Retrieved from: http://www.ceousa.org.

Crawford, J. (2004). *Educating English learners: Language diversity in the classroom* (5th ed.). Los Angeles: Bilingual Educational Services.

Cummins, J. (2001). Empowering minority students: A framework for intervention. *Harvard Educational Review, 71*(4), 649–675.

Greene, J. P. (1998). *A meta-analysis of the effectiveness of bilingual education.* Claremont, CA: Tomas Rivera Policy Institute.

Hakuta, K. (1986). *Mirror of language: The debate on bilingualism.* New York: Basic Books.

Hakuta, K. (1999). What legitimate inferences can be made from the 1999 release of SAT-9 scores with respect to the impact of Proposition 227 on the performance of LEP students? *NABE Newsletter.*

Krashen, S. D. (1996). *Under attack: The case against bilingual education.* Culver City, CA: Language Education Associates.

Krashen, S. D. (1999). *Condemned without a trial: Bogus arguments against bilingual education.* Portsmouth, NH: Heinemann.

Lambert, W. E., & Tucker, B. R. (1972). *Bilingual education of children: The St. Lambert experiment.* Rowley, MA: Newbury House.

Ma, J. (2002). *What works for the children? What we know and don't know about bilingual education.* Civil Rights Project. Cambridge MA: Harvard University.

Porter, R. (1990). *Forked tongue: The politics of bilingual education.* New York: Basic Books.

Porter, R. (1998). *The case against bilingual education.* Center for Equal Opportunity. Retrieved from: http://www.ceousa.org/porter/html.

Ramirez, D., Yuen, S., Ramey, D., & Pasta, D. (1991). Executive summary. *Final report. Longitudinal study of structured English immersion strategy, early-exit and late-exit transitional bilingual education programs for language minority children.* San Mateo, CA: Aguirre International.

Rossell, C. H. (1992). Nothing matters? A critique of the Ramirez et. al. longitudinal study. *Bilingual Research Journal, 16*(1&2), 159–186.

Rossell, C. H., & Baker, K. (1996). The educational effectiveness of bilingual education. *Research in the Teaching of English, 30*(1), 7–74.

Secada, W. G., et al. (1998). *No more excuses* (The final report of the Hispanic dropout project). Washington, DC: Office of the Undersecretary, U.S. Department of Education. Retrieved from: http://www.ncbe.gwu.edu/miscpubs/hdp/final.htm.

Snow, C. (1990). Rationales for native language instruction: Evidence from research. In A. Padilla, H. Fairchild, & C. Valadez (Eds.), *Bilingual education: Issues and strategies* (pp. 60–74). Newbury Park: Sage.

Tse, L. (2001). *Why don't they learn English? Separating fact from fallacy in the U.S. language debates.* New York: Teachers College Press.

Willig, A. (1985). A meta-analysis of selected studies on the effectiveness of bilingual education. *Review of Educational Research, 55*, 269–317.

Teaching With Linguistic and Cultural Diversity in Mind

Commins, N. L. (1989). Language and affect: bilingual students at home and at school. *Language Arts, 66*(1), 29–43.

Gay, G. (2000). *Culturally responsive teaching: Theory, research and practice.* New York: Teachers College Press.

Hense, R., Katz, A., Norte, E., Sather, S. E., & Walker, E. (2002). *Leading for diversity: How school leaders promote positive interethnic relations.* Thousand Oaks, CA: Corwin.

Hollins, E. R. (Ed.). (1996). *Transforming curriculum for a culturally diverse society.* Mahwah, NJ: Lawrence Erlbaum Associates.

Howard, G. R. (2002). *We can't teach what we don't know: White teachers, multiracial schools.* New York: Teachers College Press.

Nieto, S. (2003). *Affirming diversity: The sociopolitical context of multicultural education,* 4th ed. Boston: Allyn & Bacon.

Ovando, C., & Collier, V. (2002). *Bilingual and ESL classrooms: Teaching in multicultural contexts,* 3rd ed. New York: McGraw Hill.

Reyes, M., & Halcon, J. (Eds.). (2001). *The best for our children: Critical perspectives on literacy for Latino students.* New York: Teachers College Press.

Rodriguez, G. G. (1999). *Raising nuestros niños: Bringing up Latino children in a bicultural world.* New York: Fireside Books.

Slavin, R. E., & Calderon, M. (2001). *Effective programs for Latino students.* Mahwah, NJ: Lawrence Erlbaum Associates.

Valdés, G. (1997). Dual-language immersion programs: A cautionary note concerning the education of language-minority students. *Harvard Educational Review, 67*(3), 391–429.

Valdés, G. (1999). *Con Respeto: Bridging the distances between culturally diverse families and schools.* New York: Teachers College Press.

Valdés, G. (2001). *Learning and not learning English: Latino students in American schools.* Multicultural Education Series. New York: Teachers College Press.

Vasquez, O. A., Pease-Alvarez, L., & Shannon, S. M. (1994). *Pushing boundaries: Language and culture in a Mexicano community.* New York: Cambridge University Press.

Strategies for Second Language Instruction

Agor, B. (Ed.). (2000). *Integrating the ESL standards into classroom practice grades 9–12.* Alexandria, VA: TESOL.

Chamot, A. U., Barnhardt, S., El-Dinary, P., & Robbins, J. (1999). *Learning strategies handbook: Creating independent learners.* New York: Longman.

Chamot, A. U., & O'Malley, J. M. (1994). *CALLA Handbook: Implementing the Cognitive Academic Language Learning Approach.* Reading, MA: Addison Wesley.

Chamot, A. U., O'Malley, J., & Kupper, L. (1997). *Building bridges: Content and learning strategies for ESL.* Boston, MA: Heinle & Heinle.

Cloud, N., Genesee, F., & Hamayan, E. (2000). *Dual language instruction: A handbook for enriched education.* Boston, MA: Thomson Heinle.

Davies Samway, K. (Ed.). (2000). *Integrating the ESL standards into classroom practice grades 3–5.* Alexandria, VA: Teachers of English to Speakers of Other Languages.

Fay, K., & Whaley, S. (2004). *Becoming one community: Reading and writing with English language learners.* Portland, ME: Stenhouse.

Freeman, D. E., & Freeman, Y. S. (2001). *Between worlds: Access to second language acquisition.* Portsmouth, NH: Heinemann.

Freeman, Y. S., Freeman, D. E., & Mercuri, S. P. (2004). *Dual language essentials for teachers and administrators.* Portsmouth, NH: Heinemann.

Genesee, F. (1994). *Educating second language children: The whole child, the whole curriculum, the whole community.* Cambridge, UK: Cambridge University Press.

Hurley, S. R., & Tinajero, J. V. (2001). *Literacy assessment of second language learners.* Needham Heights, MA: Allyn & Bacon.

Irujo, S. (Ed.). (2000). *Integrating the ESL standards into classroom practice grades 6–8.* Alexandria, VA: Teachers of English to Speakers of Other Languages.

O'Malley, J. M., & Valdez Pierce, L. (1996). *Authentic assessment for English language learners: Practical approaches for teachers.* Addison-Wesley.

Smallwood, B. (Ed.). (2000). *Integrating the ESL standards into classroom practice grades Pre-K–2.* Alexandria, VA: TESOL.

Stefanakis, E. (1998). *Whose judgment counts? Assessing bilingual children, K–3.* Portsmouth, NH: Heinemann.

TESOL. (2001). *Scenarios for ESL standards-based assessment.* Alexandria, VA: Teachers of English to Speakers of Other Languages.

Planning and Differentiating Instruction in Linguistically Diverse Schools

Barnes, C. A. (2002). *Standards reform in high-poverty schools.* New York: Teachers College Press.

Bigelow, B., Harvey, B., Karp, S., & Miller, L. (Eds.). (2001). *Rethinking our classrooms, Vol. 2.* Milwaukee, WI: Rethinking Schools.

Campbell Hill, B. (2001). *Developmental continuums: A framework for literacy instruction and assessment K–8.* Norwood, MA: Christopher-Gordon.

Cole, R. (Ed.). (2001). *More strategies for educating everybody's children.* Alexandria, VA: Association for Supervision & Curriculum Development.

DuFour, R., & Eaker, R. (1998). *Professional learning communities at work: Best practices for enhancing student achievement.* Alexandria, VA: Association for Supervision & Curriculum Development.

Harmin, M. (1998). *Strategies to inspire active learning: Complete handbook.* White Plains, NY: Inspiring Strategies Institute.

Heacox, D. (2002). *Differentiating instruction in the regular classroom: How to reach and teach all learners. Grades 3–12.* Minneapolis, MN: Free Spirit Publishing.

Ingraham, P. B. (1997). *Creating and managing learning centers: A thematic approach.* Peterborough, NH: Crystal Springs Books.

Jobe, R., & Dayton-Sakari, M. (2002). *Info-Kids: How to use nonfiction to turn reluctant readers into enthusiastic learners.* Markham, Ontario: Pembroke Publishers.

Marzano, R. J., Pickering, D. J., & Pollock, J. E. (2001). *Classroom instruction that works: Research based strategies for increasing student achievement.* Alexandria VA: Association for Supervision & Curriculum Development.

Martinello, M. L., & Cook, G. E. (2000). *Interdisciplinary inquiry in teaching and learning. 2nd Edition.* Upper Saddle River, NJ: Prentice Hall.

McNaughton, S. (2002). *Meeting of minds.* Huntington Beach, CA: Learning Media.

Miller, D. (2002). *Reading with meaning: Teaching comprehension in the primary grades.* Portland, ME: Stenhouse.

Moline, S. (1995). *I see what you mean: Children at work with visual information.* Portland, ME: Stenhouse.

Morrow, L. M. (2002). *The literacy center: Contexts for reading and writing* (2nd ed.). Portland, ME: Stenhouse.

Northern Nevada Writing Project Teacher-Researcher Group. (1996). *Team teaching.* York, ME: Stenhouse.

Popham, W. J. (2001). *The truth about testing: An educator's call to action.* Alexandria, VA: Association for Supervision & Curriculum Development.

Schmoker, M. (2001). *The results fieldbook: Practical strategies from dramatically improved schools.* Alexandria, VA: Association for Supervision & Curriculum Development.

Schumm, J., Vaughn, S., & Leavell, A. (1994). Planning pyramid: A framework for planning for diverse student needs during content area instruction. *The Reading Teacher, 47*(8), 608–615.

Silver, H., Strong, R. W., & Perini, M. J. (2000). *So each may learn: Integrating learning styles and multiple intelligences.* Alexandria, VA: Association for Supervision & Curriculum Development.

Stover, L., Neubert, G., & Lawlor, J. (1993). *Creating interactive environments in the secondary school.* Washington, DC: National Education Association.

Stronge, J. (2002). *Qualities of effective teachers.* Alexandria, VA; Association for Supervision & Curriculum Development.

Tomlinson, C., & Allan, S. (2000). *Leadership for differentiating schools and classrooms.* Alexandria, VA: Association for Supervision & Curriculum Development.

Zeichner, K. M., & Liston, D. P. (1996). *Reflective teaching: An introduction*. Mahwah, NJ: Lawrence Erlbaum Associates.

Zemelman, S., Daniels, H., & Hyde, A. (1998). *Best practice: New standards for teaching and learning in America's schools* (2nd ed.). Portsmouth, NH: Heinemann.

AUTHOR INDEX

SUBJECT INDEX

A

Academic vs. social competence, 39–40
Assessment, 58, 81–86, 89–96, 102, 113, 121–122, 154–156, *see also* Standardized testing
   change in, 97–100
   documentation of growth, 96

B

Beliefs, 11, 73, 105–106, 109, 140, 142–143, 190–193, 196, *see also* Teacher philosophies
Belonging, 140–143
Bilingual education, *see also* ESL instruction
   advantages of, 145–146
   education programs, 66–71, 113–120, 123–125, 134–135
    early exit, 55
    English-only instruction, 106–113, 126, 129–130, 132–133
    pull-out, 3, 16–18, 124
    two-way immersion, 55, 77
   literacy development, 159–161

native language, 16, 43–44, 49–50, 56–57, 67, 69–70, 81, 93, 99, 113, 117, 124, 129, 132, 148, 151
primary language, roles of, 16, 43–44, 48–71, 96, 102–105, 113–114, 120, 123–125, 127–133, 143, 147–154, 167
proficiency, xiv, 104–105, 125–126, 143–146, 150–151, 156–158
subtractive bilingualism, 128, 149

C

Classroom community, 21–22, 50

D

Demographic change, ix, xiii, 34–36, 61–66, 79, 87–88

E

English for the Children, 67
English-only instruction, 106–113, 126, 129–130, 132–133